Joyful Mourning

A True Love Story

Charles G. Pedley BA MSEd

www.joyfulmourning.com

*May you be blessed as
our family has been!*

Joyful Mourning

Copyright 2013 by Charles G. Pedley
Son Media Life Publishing
SonMediaLife.com

All Rights Reserved
No part of this book may be reproduced or transmitted in any form or by any means without written permission of the author.

ISBN #9780991751730

In Appreciation, my thanks go to:

- **Gary S. Page,** teacher, preacher and author for encouraging me to write my book.
- My **daughter Rebecca** Woodworth Laird for giving me permission to publish this book from my point of view.
- **Pastor Mike Hargreaves** for being like a father to Tedd when his own father was far away
- The **People of Cumberland**, Virginia who extended their love to Tedd & Rebecca
- The **People of Shiloh New Covenant Church**, Cumberland, Virginia for their wonderful southern hospitality and love for my daughter and son-in-law
- My wife **Ellen**, cancer survivor, for her 47 years of patience with me and for making constructive criticisms of my writing.
- **Elizabeth Carden** for allowing me to include her story of meeting my daughter Rebecca and Tedd in Virginia.
- **Barrie Brown** for his intelligent editing.
- **Jamie & Martha Douglas** & **Ellen** for helping select the best design for the cover
- **Dr. Bill Gaultiere** for allowing me to use his self-tests in the Appendices
- **Dr. Tim Lowenstein** of Conscious Living Foundation for permission to include his Stress Tests
- **God** for the inspiration to write
- My grandson, **Ian Laird** for final proofing before publishing for Amazon.

Memory

Memory is a funny thing. My daughter has corrected most of my memory lapses. **However this is my point of view of what happened.** All major events are the same but there may be small points that I did not remember well but nevertheless they do not detract from this true love story.

Introduction

Please refer to my *JoyfulMourning.com* website at **http://www.joyfulmourning.com** for photos and more background information about this story. You can also read the personal experience story of one young lady, ***Elizabeth***, just entering the the youth group which Tedd and Rebecca led at Shiloh Community Church in Cumberland, Virginia.

Why Another Book on Grieving?

"Why should someone pick up your book rather than any of a myriad of other authors, most of whom are much more well-known?" Good question!

So here goes. I will try to tell you.

I believe that God put a burden on my heart to write this book even from before the time of my son–in-law's death in 1998. Even though it was over four years later when this book was begun, I still grieve the passing on of Tedd. "Oh, boy!" you say. "Another fanatic saying God told him to do something!"

Alright, if you want to believe I am a fanatic, that is okay! Remember that the short form of the word "fanatic" is "fan". *Yes, I am a proud fan of the fact that God has always wanted to speak to us, always desired our friendship. We were created by Him because He was lonely!* Read Genesis!

So, yes I am a fanatic, who believes God still wants to guide our lives, when we understand He is there and when we do NOT understand! My daughter,

Rebecca's song, **Beautiful** from her ***Broken Clay*** CD says it best.

> Lovingly He sees your tiny hand
> And dreams of all the plans He has for you
> Tenderly, His finger
> Has molded the inner parts of you
> And as each part He created
> A smile on His face, a tear in His eye
> Walking in the smallness of life
> Growing in the little things you do
> Pressing on although scared and frightened
> His gentle hand pulling you through
> He was there.
> And a lump of clay molded, fitly fashioned
> Created in the image of His son
> Your heart now beats as one with the Father's
> You're made a man, it's done
>
> Beautiful ....
> From the baby to the man
> Oh, beautiful ...
> Even though you don't understand
> Beautiful
> Meet for the Master's use
> A lump of clay in His hand
> The thoughts that He has planned
> You're an instrument in His hand
> Beautiful, so beautiful
> Beautiful

You see, when I asked God how I should pray for Tedd the last time he got sick in 1998, I had the distinct impression in my mind of the words, "**Joyful Mourning**". I did not want to believe at the time that God was telling me that Tedd was going to die, so I thought, "*No this cannot be from God.*

Why had Tedd recovered so many times, including at least one time when his heart appeared to stop, if he was just going to die anyway a few years later? I must not have heard right."

That is what I thought. But it was wishful thinking. God had been honest with me. He told me to prepare to mourn but He would still give us joy through our time of mourning, but I did not want to hear that. Who would? Even then in 2008, I would occasionally have a particularly vivid thought come back to me.

For a moment as I write this, I am there again. I am living the joys and sorrows they went through.

Yes, even though my daughter is remarried to a wonderful husband and she has three sons, Ian, MacGregor and Nathan who of course are the smartest little grandsons in the whole world! :-) I am very happy for my daughter. I love my new son-in-law and admire him very much. So why do I still grieve sometimes? Is that healthy? Shouldn't I forget the sad past?

I will discuss that later, but it is not a bad thing, unless of course it consumes my thoughts now almost fifteen years after the fact. It doesn't. But so many times we expected a miracle and it looked like God was going to give us one. A miracle of healing Tedd. But, …. I am getting ahead of my story.

Contents

1 A Miracle? 1
2 My Experiences with Grieving 9
3 Rebecca - Daughter Number Two 17
4 Tedd 25
5 The Shockwave! 35
6 -The Call 43
7 Virginia is for Lovers! 49
8 The End of New Beginnings 67
9 Rebecca the Strong 73
10 The Miracle 87
11 My Way or The Highway? 93
12 Grieving Your Loss 103
13 Body "Meet Soul and Spirit" 111
14 The Grieving Process 125
15 Coping Strategies 131
16 The Investor 143
Appendix A: Do You Have Anxiety? 153
Appendix B: Are You Depressed? 155
Appendix C: Life Stress Test 157
Appendix D: What is Your Image of God? 161
Appendix E: Do You Esteem Yourself? 165
Appendix F: Do You Overreact Emotionally? ... 167
Appendix G: What is Your Emotional IQ? 169
Appendix H: Links to Help You Cope 173
Appendix I: Mental Health & Counseling 175

1 A Miracle?

It was 11:45 P.M. July 20, 1998. The phone rang. It was my daughter, Rebecca. "Dad, the doctor said he noticed considerable improvement!"

Is this the miracle we had been waiting almost four years for? She explained that Tedd, her husband of less than four years, right now, was able to do what he had not been able to do for months. Lie down!

He had spent the last few months sitting upright in a recliner, sleeping little cat naps when he could. Lying down would have allowed the fluid around his lungs to squeeze in and choke him. His life was living in that chair. We both felt encouraged that maybe this nightmare was at an end. Maybe, Tedd was getting better! Maybe healed forever!

Tedd had been diagnosed with Stage 3 Hodgkin's Disease about six months after marrying Rebecca. It had been an ongoing battle. He had been declared free of the insidious disease twice before. Only to have it return a few months later.

Through the struggle, Rebecca and Tedd were as positive as anyone could be. During his first bout with chemotherapy, it wasn't unusual to see all the nurses gathered around his room watching Tedd and Rebecca's wedding video. I thanked our friend, Guy, the sound man for his help with the wedding, He said, "Wedding? That was no wedding! That was a production!"[1]

Rebecca and Tedd's friends at Bible college were all part of the wedding party in some way and most of them were part of the college musical group, **Servant**, including Tedd. So the ceremony was planned to capitalize on all this talent being together at one time, in one place. At appropriate points in the ceremony, there would be a pause. Then the whole wedding party would turn around and face the audience and sing! That brought tears to my eyes. It had been a most joyful event for our second daughter and for my wife, Ellen and I, even though there was the lingering thought that after the wedding, our home would never be the same again. Ellen and I would have to get to know each other all over again. All those years of experiencing family with two daughters, watching them grow, helping them mature would be gone. No one else but Ellen & I and at least one cat

---

[1]Sadly this year 2012, Guy Desjardins, passed away from cancer.

left in our home. Rebecca was our youngest of two daughters to be married and leave the nest. Her sister Ann had been married several years earlier to Jon Guinn whom she too had met at EBI, (Elim Bible Institute).

Six months passed after that most beautiful yet sad time. Tedd and Rebecca were enjoying learning to know each other as husband and wife. They were still in the 'honeymoon stage' of their marriage as the expression goes.

One morning going to work as a roofer in a suburb north of Detroit, Michigan, Tedd tried to walk up the sloped driveway. Calling up to his boss, already on the roof, he said, "I think I need to go to the hospital!" **He was not able to walk up that driveway because he was so weak.**

Even though Tedd was working as a roofer to bring in money for their little apartment in Southfield, Michigan, he was interning to be a pastor, which was his first love! A dream that had been with him since he was eleven.

It was one of those 'God-incidences' that he had chosen to intern at a 'faith church'. Now some 'faith churches' do go to an extreme believing that no one should ever be sick. The pastor of Harvest Christian, Pastor King, was not that extreme. He realized that people do get sick and die. But he also recognized that nowhere in the Bible did Jesus ever say to anyone, "***You have too much faith!***" On the contrary, Jesus often scolded his disciples by saying "***Oh ye of little faith!***" Faith is a good thing. Without faith we could not live life.

Every morning we have faith that we are not going to die in a car crash or else we would never get inside that mechanical beast. We have faith that our boss will pay us or we would never go to work. We have faith that we are not going to die tomorrow or we would spend that last day doing something more pleasurable!

Faith is a necessity of life, nothing unusual. Some think that it is unusual only when it gets connected with Christianity.

We went to sleep in high spirits believing, just maybe, that this sickness that we had all gone through was nearing an end.

It was. 2:30 A.M. July 21, 1998. Again the phone rang.

Hoping for the best but always fearing the worst, I got up to answer it. We were always conscious that the call could be bad news about our mothers, both in their 70's.

On the other end I heard, "Charles? It's Pastor Mike. Tedd has just gone to be with the Lord!" I thanked him and told him we would pack up and be there as soon as we could.

I was in stunned semi-shock. I had been told a few hours earlier that Tedd was 'considerably better'. How could this be?

I had to wake my wife, Ellen and tell my brain step-by-step, what needed doing before we could leave our home, our cat and my business. 6:30 A.M. we were packed and on the road. It was a 10 to 13 hour trip but it gave my wife and I time to talk. Time to listen to inspiring and faith-building music and time to see the beautiful countryside through five states as we travelled from our home near Niagara Falls, Ontario to one of our favourite states, Virginia!

But this trip was not going to be for building faith. This one was to be with our daughter in her time of mourning. How do you comfort a 26 year old widow? I had enough trouble talking to anyone about the loss of their loved one. Now I would have to learn quickly. I would have to be there for her. I knew God would supply the words....

We were not destroyed. We were just in mourning. Even though we had faith for his healing, we also had made allowances for the fact that he could die at any time. I had to face that stark reality almost ten years previously when Ellen had been diagnosed with lymphoma. Her chemotherapy and God's grace healed her. She has not had a single trace of cancer since.

There had been many crises along the way that we had to help my daughter live through. Not that she needed our help. She was as strong, no stronger, than anyone I had ever seen go through this kind of heartache. But no one experiences the loss of a mate without needing comfort. **The very person that you need to comfort you is not there anymore!** Family and friends are needed more than any other time except the first few years of life.

My mind went back to that Sunday, in church, when I was half-listening to our pastor and at the same time asking God, how to pray for our son-in-law. The first two times when I had asked God how to pray about this disease, I had felt immediate anger at Satan for trying to steal my daughter's new husband from her at such a young age. This time, the words that came to me were *'Joyful Mourning.'* Did that mean that Tedd was going to die? I thought, "*How could this be? Surely God would not heal him twice before, only to let him die in the end. I must be mistaken.*"

"*This could not be God telling me this!*" But just in case, I wrote the words, *'Joyful Mourning'* above Psalm 1 in my Bible. Then I got angry at Satan that he would try to take our son-in-law, Rebecca's young husband, from her. I prayed earnestly for his recovery and complete healing.

This was our hope. A hope not realized. I would have to learn *'Joyful Mourning'*. God often prepares us for the crises in our lives long before they happen. I will take a moment out from the story to show you how He did that in my life.

CHARLES G. PEDLEY

2 My Experiences with Grieving

Grieving is mourning. Are you in mourning? Are you grieving a loss? Have you ever had to mourn a loss? **The chances are that you may be experiencing grief or have experienced it and not really known it.** We all know that if we lose someone close to us, then grief will occur. But most of us **do not realize** that we can experience grief **over many different losses**.

In my own life I have had to learn to grieve:

- When my dad went blind before I started school. Have you ever played catch with a blind father?
- Because my mother had to go to work in the 50's, we moved a lot and I lost many of my best childhood friends each time we moved; none of which I have ever regained.
- After skipping Grade 2 because of high ability, I failed a year of college.
- My wife's little brother died at the age of 7.

- My wife, Ellen has about a 75% hearing loss and it is getting worse. She now requires two expensive hearing aids.
- She had lymphoma in 1987. She is a survivor.
- My dad got cancer in 1989. He passed away in 1990.
- Our family Siamese cat, raised from a kitten, died in 1997. She was an 'outspoken' member of our family. It was hard when she had to go.
- My mother-in-law had cancer. She is a survivor.
- My reputation in teaching was "on hold" for several years because of lies told about me.
- Now my wife and I are grieving the loss of our youth. Who wants to hang around an old person? At various times in our lives we always had youth gathering around us to talk, then it was young adults, then young marrieds, or new Christians. Now *we* have to be the ones to "gather around" and show an interest in those age groups or just give up and hang around with the "over-the-hill" crowd.
- Being left out. This can start when you are a kid and you are always the last one picked to

be on a team. When you become an adult, you can feel this way when no one seeks you out to talk to after church. When you hear that a bunch of the guys went canoeing but no one asked you. The choice is to give up, get bitter or overcome it by you being the one to seek people out.

Did you identify with any of these losses? There are many other losses which we may experience.
- Loss of a dream.
- Loss of a job.
- The birth of a special needs child.
- Losing someone who did not die but for one reason or another is now out of your life.
- Your children growing up and moving out to start their own lives.
- Never finding anyone to spend the rest of your life with. Having to remain single when you want to be married.

When we are teenagers or young adults we begin to dream what our lives could be like. *Did you ever dream that you would become a millionaire? A hockey star? A successful businessman owning your own corporation? Did you ever dream of becoming very successful, or travelling around the world?*

Then age 35 or 40 hits, midlife! **The gradual realization that half of your life is over and your dream has not been realized can smack you in the head like a ton of bricks.**

Or you are working your way up in a company hoping someday to be the boss and then the pink slip comes. You are fired! What a shock to a dream! Starting all over was not part of your plan!

You were going with someone with whom you wished to spend the rest of your life. Then that special person finds someone else. Or a car accident occurs suddenly robbing you of your best friend and your dreams of marriage. Now you must start again!

I must share my own experience of loss as my oldest daughter, Ann, went away to college. My wife and younger daughter Rebecca were going around the house with tears in their eyes for weeks before. *I kept trying to tell them that she wasn't dying, just going away to college!* They could not communicate with me the loss they felt. I thought they were the typical females, *too emotional!*

Then the day arrived. We drove Ann to the college, listened to the orientation session with her and then were invited to a wonderful tea and dessert reception. A lump was welling up in my spirit. I had to go outside.

I started to walk around the football field. **Suddenly, I realized that this was it!** Ann would never live at home again. All those wonderful years of helping her grow, those summer vacations we shared. They were suddenly all gone. No more driving her to swimming lessons or youth group. No more evening meals asking her how her day had been. No more of her friends invited to our house. No more teaching her to ride a bicycle or drive a car. Those days were all gone! Gone like a mist in the morning sun.

The tears came. Now I knew why they had been crying for weeks. **I knew that she would always be our daughter** *but never our little girl again!* She would graduate, find a mate and start her own family. We would never be part of her daily life again. That thought hit hard! The soft rain seemed to magnify my tears. **Even the sky was crying!**

We spend so much of our lives raising children that it becomes part of who we are. You're Mom. I'm Dad! That relationship will never change but the excitement, sometimes good, sometimes bad, of raising children and watching them grow into young adulthood is **a 'ONCE' experience.** Once it is done, the chances are that you are not going to start over raising a new family!

So can you identify with any of these experiences? Are you experiencing one loss or another? **There are many forms of grieving, none of which are things that anyone would choose.** They just happen. Life happens. And life can and will go on! The question is ... **will you**?

You *will* if you understand a few points about grieving and then make some right decisions. But first let me share what can happen if you make the wrong decisions.

I once knew a man in his fifties, but when I met him in church, he had just come back, after about 40 years of non-attendance. *What made him stay away that long?* His mother had died when he was 11. He looked at that coffin with his mother's body in it and inside told God that if that was what He was like, he was going to have NOTHING to do with Him. He made good on his promise, until 40 years later!

What brought him back? The same kinds of things in life that many of us experience. When we are young, without consciously thinking about it, we believe we are immortal. And in one way that is correct. But our bodies are not! We never think about death, our own or those of our loved ones. But **life has a way of waking us up, making us grow up, by rudely interjecting 'tragedies' into our lives.** We realize we are NOT immortal and neither are our loved ones. Our bodies eventually die. **Then we have to face our other two parts, Soul and Spirit, which we may not have met before.**

Back to the man, I will call him Wes. He had been having trouble with his eyes and had to face the fact that he may lose his sight! A 'tragedy' that woke up his soul and spirit and made him face reality. He shared with me that he had lived with forty years of bitterness bottled up inside. He was so happy that it was now all gone.

When we meet something that we can do **nothing** about in our physical selves, we are often shocked into meeting the rest of our being that we don't think much about. **Have you ever looked in the mirror and said, "My soul doesn't look too bad today!" or "Yuk! My spirit needs a makeover!"** I sincerely doubt it! We look at our bodies in the mirror and seldom think about the other, invisible, parts of us.

My hope and prayer is that this book will help you face whatever you have to face right now or in the future, help you grieve, make you realize you are not alone as much as you may feel like no one understands, and come out JOYFUL on the other side when you are done with your MOURNING!

In fact, I will go a little farther. My sincere prayer is that you will be helped to be *joyful even as you are going through mourning*.

There are many things in life which can cause grief. Many times, we do not even know we are grieving or do not want to admit it. **We do not have a choice** in the 'tragedies' that happen but we **ALWAYS** have a choice about **HOW** we grieve! **Will you let me help you grieve?**

To encourage you to see that life can go on, I would like to share the rest of the story of how my daughter, Rebecca, lost her husband when she was only 25 years old and went on to experience, *'Joyful Mourning'*.

But first I must tell you a little about Rebecca.

3 Rebecca - Daughter Number Two

Rebecca was very different from her older sister, Ann. I guess that is good! Who needs two of the same?

When Rebecca and Ann were young children, I would try to teach them to be unselfish and share. I would offer Ann a taste of my ice cream cone and she would accept. Then I would ask for a taste of hers and she would hold out her cone so I could get my lick.

But with Rebecca sometimes it would go a different way, not always the way it did with Ann.

Rebecca was always an energetic bundle of joy which God was beginning even then to make into an individual who knew her own mind and was not going to let others change it! To some that is pure 'stubbornness'. **But when the going gets rough, stubbornness quickly becomes perseverance. It becomes strong will!**

And that is exactly what Rebecca needed!

When Rebecca was a child, she would often play with her toys, her doll house, her castle or her large bear in the living room while merrily singing to herself. After a bit we would not hear a sound and hurry to the living room to find Rebecca draped over whatever toy she had been playing with **fast asleep**. She always enjoyed every moment of her waking hours until she had no energy left to stay awake and would just fall asleep.

She may have inherited my energy level as I am much the same, stubbornly staying up when I should be in bed, trying hard to finish up some project even when my brain has already started to fall asleep.

I am telling you all of these things because **every experience we go through in life, is there for a reason,** often that we do not understand. Good and bad. Happy and sad. All help to develop our inner strengths and form our most unique personalities.

Rebecca was always slim. Somehow or other, she often succumbed to childhood illnesses. When she was away from school, a mean little girl who was supposed to be her best friend would tell other kids lies about Rebecca. When she came back to school, everyone would turn their back on Becky, believing the lie they had been told. Eventually, she just told the 'best friend' off and made up her mind that she was going to have fun anyway even if she had to have it by herself!

God took her in His loving hand and allowed the sadness of a child being separated from her friends and turned it into strength to be an individual, no matter what the odds.

Later on, we decided when the 'best friend' stole from her desk during her absence, that maybe she needed a change of environment. So we switched her to the school where I was teaching.

I had a 'royal pain' kind of a guy in my classroom that year. I was always getting complaints from the Grade 7 or 8 girls that Chris was being a 'pervert'. When I questioned them about it, I discovered he was making lewd or pornographic comments to them or pulling their bra straps when I wasn't looking. On occasion, 'girly' magazines were found falling out of his desk. He was a pest that had to be dealt with constantly.

Then after this bully pestered Rebecca for many days outside on the playground, he decided to get pushy. He was one year older, a male and must have outweighed her by at least fifty pounds but that did not stop him from attempting to push Rebecca off a hill of snow. He partially succeeded.

When Rebecca recovered her balance she pushed him right back. **Catching him off guard, he fell into a pile of snow at the bottom.** I believe that was the last time that he attempted to pick on her. He had met his match even though his match was at least one year younger, much lighter, and a girl to boot! That's often the way it is with bullies. When someone stands up to them, they give up. Again, God was strengthening this young lady's character. I could cite many occurrences like these, but I believe you get the picture.

As she got older, she gradually learned to be more sharing and thoughtful of others, especially boys! Rebecca never had much trouble attracting friends of the opposite sex. We told her she couldn't date until she was 35 or out of our home on her own. It was a joke to fend off the inevitable question all teens ask, "*When can I date?*"

Rebecca became very interested in photography. So, when she graduated from high school we bought her a good 35mm camera. Already with her artistic bent displayed since she was a little girl, she had become quite good with a snapshot camera. She honed her skills, took a college course at night and was all set to attend a school which had a reputation for the best photography courses. She had dreams of opening her own photography business. **However, a series of events occurred that led her in a totally different direction.** God was at the helm of her ship steering her in the direction He wanted her to go!

She applied to the school and they told her that she would need to submit a portfolio of her photography. So, Rebecca got it all together and waited for the letter to arrive to bring it to Sheridan College, about one hour away. Late August arrived, but no letter! Finally, she phoned the college and asked about submitting her work. **They told her the shocking news that the course was filled!** She told them she had been waiting for their letter and had never received it. Later she discovered that her name and another person's address somehow got mixed up and her letter went to someone in Ottawa, 300 miles away!

So now what? Well, she had been working part-time since she was 15, so she applied for and got a job at a dress shop in the mall. She worked at this for several months and without us saying a word, she started to pay for a lot of her own clothing and the fancy hair conditioners and sprays young ladies learn to love.

This young lady who I had thought as a child had exhibited selfish traits **was proving she was not the person I once thought she was**! Then a missionary from Thailand came to our church to share his experiences about the needy people with whom he worked. Rebecca was deeply touched by the hopelessness of their condition. **She decided she wanted to go somewhere, anywhere and help others who were less fortunate than she had been**. We suggested she try our denomination's reach-out-to-Israel program called 'Kibbutz Shalom', a mission to reach out to the Israeli people. She applied and was accepted. She read all the orientation literature and was ready to go for final training early the next year in February of 1992.

But Saddam Hussein invaded Kuwait and started lobbing scud missiles at Israel. Everyone waited to see what would happen but the time came and went for the trip and the call came to inform her it had been put off indefinitely because it was too unsafe at this time.

God must have been tugging at her heart because she went back to work at the ladies shop but could not forget about what she had seen and heard from the missionary. She decided that maybe she would go to Bible school for one year and then re-apply at Sheridan the following year. That August we packed up the car, Guinness-Book-of-Records-style and drove her to Elim Bible Institute for her one year of Bible college. This was the same college where her older sister, Ann had attended and come home with a husband! (Well, not quite that quickly! But she got married shortly after graduation.)

One year stretched into three in short order! And at EBI, Elim Bible Institute, the nickname is, *'Elim Bridal Institute'*. Many young ladies meet their life-mates there. Rebecca was no exception. At least we thought so!

CHARLES G. PEDLEY

4 Tedd

When Rebecca brought Tedd home from Bible college for the weekend, I remember trying to make conversation with him. I asked loads of questions, but the answers were short and to the point. It was hard to get him to talk. I was curious about what she saw in him. That was revealed in due course.

I came to find out that Tedd was much more outgoing in his own element. I discovered this one time when we went to pick up Rebecca to bring her home for the weekend. Tedd was a good-looking young man. But when we saw him interacting with other students at the Bible school, he was taking time to talk to students, more specifically females, who were not the most drop-dead gorgeous nor the most popular ones. He was being a friend to those who did not have many, especially male, friends.

He was showing an interest in these people that many would not bother with. That was the first clue to me that there was more to Tedd than those short answers indicated. I was surprised because I had tried to draw Tedd out and failed,

but at school, HE WAS THE ONE drawing others out. I imagined Jesus doing exactly the same thing if He had been there. I guess He was!

>>>>>>>>><<<<<<<<<

I discovered later what an incredible hard worker Tedd was as he took a night job at a nearby factory during Bible school and barely made it back in time for breakfast and sometimes only an hour or two to sleep before going to classes. I also came to realize that our first impressions are sometimes ridiculously wrong!

>>>>>>>>><<<<<<<<<

Several years later, I got the next surprise. I put together a computer for him and he churned out a full-year's plan for youth activities, and a teaching on the Holy Spirit that was much more than surface depth.

>>>>>>>>><<<<<<<<<

When Tedd wanted to talk with me before their marriage, he did it the old-fashioned way by asking if it was okay for him to ask Rebecca to marry him. That takes so much more guts than some modern marriages. When I said, "yes". He said, "You like me!" I said "Of course," but even

though I did not know him as well as my daughter, I trusted her choice for a husband.

>>>>>>>>><<<<<<<<<

When he and Rebecca finally received a call to go to a little country church in Cumberland, Virginia despite the cancer that was in remission, he asked us if we wanted to come to youth group. It had been a long time since we had been asked that! He insisted that the youth wouldn't mind at all if we sat at the back and observed.

I was so surprised when suddenly this guy that I originally could not engage in conversation stepped up to the mike and said, "***Are you ready to meet with God?***" Receiving only a mild response, he said it louder, **"Are YOU READY to meet with God?"** This drew a louder response, but not enthusiastic enough for Tedd, so he yelled, **"ARE YOU READY TO MEET WITH GOD?"** This time the youth group of about 30 members almost lifted the roof off the church! This was certainly not my first impression of Tedd! First impressions are often wrong.

Time was soon to show what strength he had within him.

Here was Tedd sitting in a recliner, where he also slept, and Pastor Mike said, "Tedd you are supposed to preach on July 5th, next Sunday, so what do you want to do?" Tedd, who had previously been told by the doctors that he would be dead by July 4th, said, "You're giving me the choice of dying on the fourth or preaching on the 5th? I'll take the fifth!" This was an amendment that the creators of the U.S. Constitution could *never* have envisioned!

Now in Tedd's weakened state where it was usually a struggle for him to say a sentence, I thought the best he could do would be to share a five minute message. I noticed a few words written down on paper before the service but there could not have been more than five or six.

It was time for the message. Tedd had to be wheeled up front in his wheelchair with his friend **Pastor Tim** from Detroit, and my son-in-law, **Jon** handling the oxygen tanks that went everywhere with him. He was ready to begin. Silence filled the air. What would this young man, all skin and bones, say?

I could not believe that he preached for over 45 minutes, sharing his testimony. In Bible school he saw his roommate so in love with God and at that time,

Tedd did not have that intimate relationship even though he had known God for years. He wanted it! He sought God and God revolutionized his life and gave him a more personal relationship and a new direction.

The oxygen tanks had to be changed. Then here was my 'quiet' son-in-law, not able to breathe on his own, preaching this dynamic personal message, challenging us all to get to know God as our best friend. When no one else can comfort us, God **can and will** if we let Him. I could hardly believe that those five or six words written down on a piece of paper produced that stirring message! This was so obviously a message straight from Tedd's heart and from the heart of God!

At one point, he was telling the congregation how fantastic the youth were and he said, "**This youth group is to die for**!" And then realizing what he had said, "**I guess not a very good choice of words!**" That message was to be his last and I am sure he knew it. He passed away into the 'lap of God' 15 days later. His last words were, as his brother wished him goodnight, "**I've got to go now! They need me on stage. I've got to get my beat!**" (Tedd was a superb drummer.) And he made the sound and motions of beating his invisible drums with unseen drumsticks. **Forty-five minutes later he was gone. But his message is still here.**

Do you have someone to comfort you? I hope you do. But if you don't or if you need more comfort than another human can give you, I suggest you get to know the one who comforted my son-in-law, so close to death so many times for almost four years.

He went through chemotherapy and emergency operations to relieve the pressure of fluid around his heart. His heart appeared to stop at least once for what seemed like forever. He went through a bone marrow transplant, where all the white blood cells are killed off in preparation for giving the new bone marrow. He was in a state as near death as any living person can come. But through it all, he had a supernatural spirit of optimism.

I still remember being at their interning church in Detroit, on a Sunday, when Pastor King, said to the congregation, "*I went into the hospital to cheer up Tedd this week. But he cheered me up instead!*" A few weeks later when Tedd was out of the hospital and healing again, Pastor King asked him to preach on a Wednesday night. He preached on **'The Secret Place'**. That place you can go to when no earthly being can bring you comfort, but God can. (Psalm 91:1)

You can crawl up on that big lap of God and curl up in His arms, enjoying His presence, as you may have done with your dad or mom when you were a young child. Why not? God is our father! An excerpt from Rebecca's song, '**Tell Him, Father**' expresses this relationship better than I can say.

> *"Won't you tell him, Father*
>
> *As he nuzzles in your great big lap, say for me*
>
> *Your fingers running through his hair*
>
> *No more trouble anywhere...*
>
> *Won't you tell him that I love him?"*

This was written as a part of her grieving process a few months after Tedd died. She could no longer talk to Tedd, but she COULD talk to God! And couldn't God remind Tedd how much she missed him?

And that brings us to Psalm 139. Have you read that Psalm? I have heard the verses many times and they have always inspired me.

> **Psalm 139:15-16** WEB
> *15. My frame wasn't hidden from you, When I was made in secret, woven together in the depths of the earth.*
> *16. Your eyes saw my body.* **In your book they were all written, The days that were ordained for me, When as yet there were none of them.**

The last several years since Tedd's death, these words have taken on a special place in my life. But I am getting ahead of my story. How about Rebecca, his wife, our daughter? How did she survive all of this? How did she keep on living when the man she expected to spend her life with was diagnosed with Stage 3 Hodgkin's disease within 6 months of their wedding? How did she keep on going when 3 days before their fourth anniversary Tedd left this earth to be with God?

I hope you will be encouraged that there is hope when you read my daughter's story. In fact, with God, there is MORE than HOPE there is CERTAINTY!

And now, back to the beginning.

CHARLES G. PEDLEY

5 *The Shockwave!*

The phone rang. It was Rebecca, phoning from Detroit. They had just received the news.... Tedd had Hodgkin's disease!

There is NOTHING more heart-rending than seeing your child go through hardship. Yes, she was an adult of 22 and he was 23 but they were still our children. I think it would be easier to experience the pain yourself than have your child go through it.

When Becca and Ann, her older sister, were young, we could just put a Band-Aid on their hurts and say a few comforting words to make them forget about it, **but what do you say to a young couple in the prime of life when the husband is diagnosed with cancer?** When he is faced with the distinct possibility of death after only six months of marriage? There is no Band-Aid, no trite little word of encouragement offered without much thought that can make that hurt go away! This kind of choice confronting us could have either made us bitter or better! **The choice was ours; Ellen's, mine,**

Rebecca's and most of all Tedd's, the one who had the most to lose.

Tedd and Rebecca's natural and supernatural optimism were certainly a help, as were the prayers of the strong faith church where they were interning to be pastors. But no amount of natural optimism would have carried them through this ordeal!

Here was Tedd, newly married, unable to earn any income because he had to be in the hospital for chemotherapy. God provided Rebecca with a waitress job at a quaint little restaurant for a while. Tedd's health care plan with his employer was about to be cancelled because Tedd could not seek work until he had recovered from the chemotherapy.

Imagine that! I thought that you paid health care premiums to provide for emergencies when you couldn't work because of poor health! But no, apparently I was mistaken. The plan only applied if Tedd was working or actively seeking work.

Being Canadian we were not used to 'U.S – style' health care plans. If Tedd had been Canadian, his medical needs would be paid for by our national health care plan, but he was not. Friends tried to help arrange unemployment insurance. But even though

Tedd had paid into the plan, since he was not actively seeking employment, he would receive no help from that source either. He fell between the cracks in the system. Without a lot of help from their church, from us, their family and from other anonymous individuals, they would not have been able to keep their modest apartment in Southfield Michigan. ***Is this how some become street people?***

But the church and various individuals within the church took them on as a ministry. For months their apartment rent was paid. The church people filled their cupboards to overflowing with food. When they needed extra help, our church, in Canada, put out a call and an offering was taken to help with the expenses.

At other times, Ellen and I gladly paid the rent. No one wanted to see this young couple abandoned. What if they had no church family? No family to help? No support system? They would have had no choice but to live on the streets.

When the chemotherapy was all over, Rebecca looked at the year's income which had been less than $12,000. Out of that amount came payments for rent, their car, plus insurance and

all those other expenses connected with owning an automobile. They had food on their plates and in their cupboard. God had provided all of their needs through their family and church friends.

Tedd had gone through the chemo with flying colours. In a few months, he was given a CAT scan. **No trace of the disease was found!** Even while Tedd was receiving chemo, he worked a desk job at an insurance company and then later when he was a bit stronger, worked for Nabisco restocking stores.

It looked like life was on track again. Little did we know.

In the meantime, Becca had to leave the restaurant where she had been working. Soon a friend mentioned an opportunity at a local bank. It just happened to be the bank where Tedd and Rebecca already did their banking. The bank had benefits such as a health plan.

Would the health care plan include Tedd with his pre-existing condition? The manager did not think so, but my daughter, not satisfied, checked all the fine print. She could find nothing about excluding pre-existing conditions! She phoned the company to be absolutely sure. **No, Tedd would not be excluded** *because of his condition! A little miracle worth over one hundred thousand dollars!*

The summer of 1995! Tedd and Rebecca were able to join us at a rented cottage on Manitoulin Island. Tedd and I played golf in the bright clear Manitoulin air! Life was great! The future looked as bright as the sky!

Then fall came! I always loved October with its bright fall colours and crisp leaves to walk through and even though November could be a bland, gray time, it was my birthday month! It was in fact my mother-in-law's birthday month. We have the same birthday, November 18. So, it was a celebration time. **But then the news came.**

Tedd was not feeling well. A checkup showed that the cancer was back! This time the only logical choice was a bone marrow transplant. His family out west all had their compatibility checked. No match! A relatively new method was being developed that showed promise. Tedd was to have intense chemotherapy, then his own bone marrow would be taken, frozen at absolute zero, (-273^0 C) and would be given back to him after high dose chemotherapy. **Apparently it is so strong that about 25% of the** *patients die from the intense chemotherapy.* His recovery chances were rated at slightly less than 50%. **It would have been higher than 50% if there was a donor who matched his blood type. Unfortunately no matching donors were found.**

Throughout this time, Tedd had one of the best cancer doctors in the United States. *He just 'happened'* **to be heading up a cancer treatment centre in Botsford hospital about 5 minutes from where they lived. And their family doctor,** *just 'happened'* **to have been one of Dr. Gordon's acquaintances. so Dr. Gordon agreed to take on Tedd.** What if they had decided that God was calling them to be missionaries in Africa and had gone there before the cancer struck? Instead of five minutes to the hospital it would have been five days! But there was an unseen plan.

Tedd went through the bone marrow treatment with flying colours. He tied the release record of 12 days after Day 0, the day when all of your white blood cells are dead. Then they started, intravenously, to give him back his purified bone marrow. He was allowed to go home even though he would have to wear a mask whenever he was out in public and spend many hours resting each day.

100 days. Another CAT scan! It came back clear! Their life was on track again! Tedd could look for a job as a pastor as his internship was almost complete! Celebration time again!

The only slight hint that all was not well was a tiny lump that Tedd still had near his throat. But it was assumed to be scar tissue and would perhaps eventually disappear.

That fall Tedd started sending out resumes to apply for a job as a youth pastor. He was regaining his strength. It was discouraging for a while. *Who wanted a pastor with cancer in remission and a possible death sentence over his head?* **It would take a very special group of people to see beyond the cancer!** God had already planned who that group would be!

CHARLES G. PEDLEY

6 *The Call*

Tedd continued to send resumes to churches where he thought he might fit in. Now one thing you DON'T INCLUDE in your resume is that you have cancer which is not cured! Can't you just see it?

> **Experience**: *Two years as a cancer patient. Experienced in receiving intense chemotherapy which makes your hair fall out, not to mention all the other side-effects. Have gone through bone marrow treatment. Cancer could still come back at any time.*

No, not quite what a resume is all about! But Tedd knew that he must tell any pastor who called him. A pastor from Alabama called. He had heard great things about Tedd. After talking to Tedd, he wanted him to come and was sure the church board would agree to hire him.

They waited all day for the phone call. Finally late at night after a long meeting, the pastor phoned. "Tedd, I really want you to come! But the board has some hesitation because of the cancer .**Questions** like **"What would happen if you got sick again? What effect would that have on the people? Would you still be able to do your job?"** were asked.

Questions like this could not be answered. But there was the answer staring them right in the face. So much hope had been built up. The position sounded just right. But the cancer won again! I was upset at the time. I thought this church believed in miracles! Couldn't they see past the sickness? Why couldn't they just hire him and trust God?

In retrospect, I see God's loving hand! Alabama was a long two days drive from Fonthill, Ontario. There would be no long-weekend visits. It would have taken two days to drive down and two days to drive back. Most long weekends have only three days! It would have made it a short visit when it required *four* days of driving! If they had been hired in Alabama, we would not see them until Christmas, then March break and then the summer.

So God took what **I thought was the poor decision of a church board** and made it into something good. We had been spoiled when they lived in Detroit. We visited every month. And when the crises came, I could take one day off school, drive my wife there to encourage them and then drive home that night, ready for school the next day. I didn't own a Lear jet so Alabama would not have allowed us that closeness.

Tedd was still getting stronger, although not as fast as he would have liked. November came. No cancer! Winter passed. **Spring arrived with a new hope. Perhaps all this sickness was past!**

Then a call came from Pastor Mike Hargreaves in Cumberland, Virginia. He had read Tedd's resume and liked what he saw. References had been checked and Pastor Mike was impressed. They needed a youth leader and associate pastor. They needed someone who was good at reaching out to the youth, but also to the community. Would Tedd and Rebecca fly down at the church's expense to preach for the church? Their hearts leaped! **Our hearts jumped for joy when we heard.** On track again! The cancer had NOT WON! There was no sign of it, except for the few small lumps which were assumed to be scar tissue. Tedd was much stronger every month!

As a family, we had always loved Virginia. The motto reads, '**Virginia is for lovers**!' Well, we loved Virginia! Those beautiful Blue Ridge Mountains! The cool Skyline Drive winding around the green and rocky summits giving breath-taking views of the Shenandoah Valley below! The smoky-blue ranges of other mountains in the distance, toward West Virginia! **Each succeeding mountain chain, as seen from the Skyline, lighter and lighter shades of blue, eventually becoming lost in the mist at the horizon, blending into the pale blue sky**.

But what a view! The Shenandoah River snaking through the valley over three thousand feet below. River of folk songs! And the state of **The Waltons**! My daughters had grown up listening to John-boy's stories. (I guess I should say, Earl Hamner's) What a beautiful state! And we could drive there easily in ONE DAY! **Another God-incident!**

On the long weekend in May, 1997 the church paid their flight to Virginia. A good sign! It was a small but growing church of about 150 and yet they not only paid Tedd's way but Rebecca's as well! If they weren't saints already, they were getting close in my mind! We waited excitedly for the weekend to end and hear the call from Detroit! **They wanted him!** *In fact after hearing Tedd, one of the parents said, "It is obvious this young man has a call on his life. I* *don't care if he only preaches 6 months to my kids! I want them to hear him!"*

Little did we know how prophetic this statement was to be.

CHARLES G. PEDLEY

7 *Virginia is for Lovers!*

This motto, seen on license plates and bumper stickers took on a new meaning for us. We loved Virginia and it seemed **Virginia also loved our family!** Now that is the best kind of love!

One of Ellen's best friends in the church, Caroline, had turned to her in January, 1997 after church and said, ***"I just feel like God is telling me that your family has been through a lot but 1997 is to be a year of blessing!"***

How right she was! We found out in January that we were to expect our first grandchild that summer! Rebecca's older sister, Ann was expecting! Very convenient since as a teacher finished with updating courses, the summer was always free. One year left to go before early retirement for me. And now the joyful job of packing up Detroit and moving it to Virginia! The church in Detroit, Harvest Christian Fellowship, gave them a wonderful send-off! .....

Detroit winters, with their bone-chilling cold winds, snow and ice, and reminders of cancer

were to be gone! They had to give way to the healing warmth of sunny Virginia! I felt strongly that if this young, slim couple were to move south that all the reminders of cancer returning each November, would be thoughts of the past. The warmth of Virginia would supply the faith to finally kill this vicious disease once and for all. And Tedd *was* feeling much better.

On first getting out of the hospital after the bone marrow treatment, he had to wear a mask whenever he was in public to prevent his weakened immune system from contracting any germs. He could not even go into a restaurant for a while. He could not eat raw vegetables for fear they may harbour germs which could kill him since it would take months, years even to regain his full immune system again. Their whole apartment had to be steam-cleaned before Tedd could come home. Every precaution to prevent even the tiniest infection which could become a harbinger of death for Tedd had to be taken.

I loved those Saturday morning Denny's Grand Slam breakfasts with Tedd, when he was able to take the mask off and go with me again. We always went to Best Buy after breakfast; Tedd to the music department and me to computers. After only an hour or so he'd say, "Dad, I'm tired. Can we go?" And so we'd go home to their apartment in Southfield, just north of the Detroit border.

It was all connected anyway, one giant city where you could shop any hour of the day or night! I remember my first night there, being awakened almost every hour by sirens. Police sirens, fire sirens, ambulance sirens! Sirens, sirens, sirens! So much noisier than quiet Fonthill, a town that rolls up the carpets and closes down to go home and be with the family at 6 P.M. each night, except of course, Friday.

And now that was to be the past! Virginia called! Tedd answered! Life was good again! I could not wait the few weeks until the end of June. It was such a happy time! The last day of school! A quick drive to Detroit to help Tedd finish packing and load up the Uhaul. There was not much packing to do. Tedd had stayed up every night until 2 A.M. for the past week because he was so excited he couldn't sleep anyway. We picked up the truck. His friends from the church showed up and in a few hours the truck was full and we were anxious to leave Detroit!

About a week earlier, Rebecca had driven to our place and after staying a day or so, left with my wife to be there in Attleboro in case Ann gave birth early.

There had been blessings in Detroit. Both Tedd and Rebecca learned so much from their senior pastors, Pastor King and his wife. What wonderful coaches, examples and substitute parents they had been! They were so practical. They helped Tedd and Rebecca work out a budget. Pastor King did their taxes for them since pastoral taxes are NOT an easy thing to do. The pastors and the church had blessed them with all kinds of love! Cupboards full of food! Rent paid! Car payments taken care of. The confidence of the church that Tedd would be healed had helped them through those dark days. And he was! Over and over again when it looked like he should die he didn't. They would miss their friends and mentors, but Virginia was fully prepared with new friends and new mentors! Happy days were here again!

The next morning, after a delicious breakfast, we headed out of the city. I asked Tedd several times, when he was awake if he wanted to drive. He drove only a few hours of the long trek east and then south. He slept most of the way. About 8 PM we phoned

Pastor Mike from Pennsylvania and told him that we had a few hours left to go. We were just leaving southern Pennsylvania, heading through Maryland, for Washington and then south to Richmond, Virginia.

He said, "No problem! I'll be here at the church when you arrive."

I often looked over at my tired son-in-law. He was sleeping so much. It reminded me too much of those days when he was working as a roofer in Detroit and had come home so bone-tired. I advised him as soon as he qualified for health insurance through his job to go and see the doctor, just in case. Better to nip things in the bud than take a chance. **Little did I know that this "bud" would not succumb to nipping!**

I do not know how I had the strength to drive from about 10:30 in the morning until 1 A.M. the next morning, with Tedd driving maybe once. But somehow the expectation of the great times coming for Tedd and Rebecca and for us as a family gave me all the strength I needed.

He looked so much like a little boy needing the comfort of a father next to him as he slept in the truck.

Since I had never had a son, it was a privilege to be there for him.

I loved my daughters and was very proud of the beautiful adults they had become. They had been "tomboys" before the full onset of puberty which allowed me some of the pleasures of having 'surrogate sons'. I know his own father would have been there if he could. But thousands of miles and hundreds of dollars which they did not have, separated his parents, from their oldest son.

Tedd and Rebecca had seen them once since their wedding in 1992. His parents sent them plane tickets to come out west to Washington state to see them after the initial 100 days after the bone marrow treatment had passed. The rest of the time, it was our privilege to fill in for them since a four to five hour drive is all that separated us from the "kids".

What a trip! What a blessing to help this young couple start their life-goal of ministry! I was a very blessed man! Behind the truck, we pulled a car trailer with my Mercury Villager on it.

Once the furniture was safely settled in their new house in Cumberland, Tedd and I had to drive to Massachusetts to be there for the arrival of his first nephew and our first grandson! Miles of constricted highway under summer re-construction slowed us down. Arriving on the outer beltway of Washington D.C. at twilight, about 9:30 P.M., was not exactly my fondest memory of the drive. How come so many people were up driving at that time of night? It was Saturday night. I guess others were celebrating the end of their week as we were celebrating the end of one phase of Tedd and Rebecca's lives and the exciting beginning of another!

As we pulled onto quiet Highway 60, on the outskirts of suburban Richmond and headed west at about midnight, there was a deer standing nonchalantly right beside the four lanes. It was standing in front of a car dealership, in the middle of suburbia! It looked up as if to say, *"Why aren't you in bed? I wasn't expecting company at this hour of the night! I just had to munch some of this yummy grass. It is so green. Must be those funny things that pop up out of the ground and start spraying! We don't have those out in the country! Our grass gets so dry this time of the year. It's the heat you know. Sometimes over 100, often in the 90's and cooling to 80's at night is the norm here."*

When we arrived at Shiloh New Covenant Church, at about 1 A.M., the trip had ended, but we eagerly looked forward to new beginnings. Pastor Mike was there true to his word, with the ever-present coffee cup in hand.

"Would you like a coffee? It's fresh!" Pastor Mike never allowed coffee to get stale. The pot was usually empty within the hour after being made. He was a good-looking, medium-sized man with a strong body and face. He looked the part of someone who had had military training. *He was very friendly to us both,* **but showed a devotion to Tedd.** He soon put us up at the Cumberland Motel next door for the night. We were to meet him about 9 the next morning to look at possible places for Tedd and Rebecca to settle down.

At 6:30 A.M., even though my night had been short, I sat up wide awake! Tedd was dead to the world. I didn't want to disturb him, but my stomach, as usual, said, "Eat!" I quietly unloaded the van from the car transport and drove west on Route 60. After what seemed like quite a few miles with nothing but trees on each side of the road, the occasional driveway and house, I saw the sign, "**Welcome to Cumberland**

C.H." What was C.H? I didn't find out until later that C.H. stands for Court House in Virginia. Many small communities grew up around the county court house and so everyone knew what C.H. meant, *except for strangers from the north!*

I saw a neon sign which read "**Restaurant, Open 24 hours**". I pulled up in front and wondered why there were no lights on. An attendant at the gas station, not far away explained as I bought my first delicious cappuccino from their machine, that the restaurant opens at 7 A.M. I would not have to wait long for breakfast. I guess 24 hours in the village of Cumberland means something different from gigantic Detroit where many stores never close. Tedd had even shown me once where they had all night car sales, in case you wanted to shop for one after midnight!

What a contrast! Cumberland, though smaller than Fonthill, where my wife and I lived, was much the same. **Detroit on the other hand never slept. It was always restless**. One difference I noticed at that time, was that Fonthill did not have anything open for 24 hours! But the combined gas station, convenience centre, snack-bar of Cumberland **was open!**

After breakfast, I went back to the motel and woke Tedd up. Almost 9! He got up and showered. Pastor Mike drove us around in his pickup with the windows down so we could enjoy the 'air-conditioning' of the 90°F weather outside. After looking at various apartments and houses, we drove up the rural gravel road which led to a large two and one-half story farmhouse.

There was a smaller bungalow on the other side of the driveway. The extra house that had obviously been built years ago for the hired man was a welcoming sight. It was a good-sized house with the sun streaming in the windows in the morning, three small bedrooms, a large kitchen-dining room and an equally large living room. It even had two bathrooms!

The sign on the driveway said "**Popular Springs**". As a teacher I wondered if they meant "poplar". Many people mix up the spelling of the two words. Thirty-four plus years of teaching had taught me that. However I did not notice any springs.

Tedd settled. The house looked cheery and was much larger than the small one-bedroom apartment in Detroit. There was plenty of room to have youth meetings in the living room and a large country yard outside to play games. He phoned Rebecca and she said, "Go for it!"

Pastor Mike, Jerry, a man from the church, Tedd and I emptied the truck in less time than it taken a dozen people in Detroit to load it! What a happy day!

That night, we were put up at the '*Johnson Motel*', the residence of the local pharmacist, one of the elders of the church. They were away visiting but had asked Pastor Mike to give us the run of the house, help ourselves to food and make ourselves at home. Tedd and I went to sleep in the same room, but when I woke up he was gone! I looked around. There he was fast asleep in the next bedroom. I guess those short nights had caught up with me. I fell asleep first and Tedd, kept awake by my snoring, could not sleep, so he changed rooms.

It was a house, not a motel, but it developed that nickname due to the southern hospitality of its owners. It was always available to anyone stopping by on their way through Cumberland or visiting. Ellen and I were to spend many nights there in the next year, 1998, with the frequent visits we made.

It was Sunday! The first one for me and the second for Tedd. Pastor Mike honoured Tedd by introducing him and asking the congregation to say out loud what his name was. When they answered in unison, "Tedd!" He playfully but firmly scolded them and made them say **'Pastor Tedd'**. And then reminded them, "Now don't you forget that!"

It was a beautiful, small church with 3 large windows with semicircular tops. The whole interior had been covered with cedar planking installed at a 45° angle. The outside was painted the characteristic white of Virginia houses. Of course, we were to find out later, the church, in Virginia style had been built by the members and Pastor Mike in particular.

Sitting in a clearing by the side of the highway, overlooking a pond made to collect water to supply the church, and a back field cut out of the bush, it looked like a friendly country church which it definitely was! **The only church in Cumberland having whites and a few blacks worshiping together!**

Even though separate churches had been done away with by law many years ago, rural Virginia while not obviously prejudiced against blacks maintained its multitude of separate country churches.

It was either a black church or a white church, not both. But Shiloh's motto became "**Breaking Down the Walls**". And it was attempting to do that!

A careful look at the back field showed many wildflowers and a few gravestones. The church had started its own cemetery there. It was a young church which had started in people's homes. So there were only one or two stones and at least one cross made of wood to honour the remembrance of a loved one. I counted three graves but all too soon it was due to be expanded.

Later on that Sunday, we decided to make the next long trek to Massachusetts leaving at about supper time and expecting to arrive sometime in the early morning hours. We assumed that we would miss a lot of drive-time traffic by traveling in the evening. We had to pass through Richmond, Washington, Philadelphia and New York City not to mention other smaller cities. So the trip started! My first grandson could have arrived at any time!

At Philadelphia, about 9 PM, stuck on a bridge with no way to exit I-95, we just sat and waited for a long time. Finally we moved again. So much for missing traffic! ***The next adventure was my first unexpected visit to New York City.***

We skirted New York City by exiting I-95, and traveled on I-287 out and around the city, a longer route but avoiding the centre of the city which I assumed would still be very busy at about midnight. The only thing we didn't know is that summer construction had narrowed all lanes on I-287 for miles. So we were stuck behind slow-moving trucks, sometimes having to overlap the passing lane. This did not give us much confidence to pass. It was going to take a little longer than we thought.

Now, with apologies to my American friends I have never liked American highway signs. They seem to remind you ***once*** where the upcoming exit will take you. You have to read this sign quickly, digest and memorize all the information to figure out if that is where to turn off. Then when the exit sign comes, there is only an exit number! Was this the exit we were to take to get back on I-95? I couldn't remember what exit the sign said. Maybe it was but.... And to make it worse, the highway became a 'low-way' cut into the rock and at the same time, turning constantly so that even in the headlights, you could not see more than a few hundred feet ahead. I saw a glimpse of a sign saying something about New England but had no time to read it all as the sign passed back into the darkness.

I had a funny feeling that we had missed the exit back to I-95 and when I saw the sign on an overpass, 'Welcome to Yonkers' I was sure that Yonkers was not far from the centre of New York City! What should I do? Fearing I might exit and enter a dangerous section of the city I just kept driving.

Finally I saw a commercial van pulling off towards a well-lit gas station. I followed. When they stopped I asked for directions. My fears had been right. I had missed the exit. The only choice was to keep going right down to the George Washington Bridge and then turn **left** to head toward New England. If I got into the right lane by mistake I would be forced to cross the bridge right into the centre of New York City. A place I had never seen before, except for the traffic jams on television!

To shorten the story, we made the correct turn and headed to Massachusetts. Tedd still did not feel much like driving so a few times I tried to take a few minutes nap at a service centre. Finally, after many compulsory rest breaks, we arrived in Massachusetts at about 5 A.M.

No sign of any grandson yet. In fact in spite of having a great visit, after waiting for almost a week Tedd and Rebecca felt they had to leave to take up their duties at Shiloh. Nathaniel was born during the next week.

Later on that summer before I went back to teach my final, pre-retirement year, we paid a visit to Virginia to see how they were settling in. One day after we arrived, Tedd took some flex time off and we went into Farmville to play golf. **Here was Tedd, a cancer patient who had NOT been declared totally well, playing 9 holes of golf in the 95^0 F Virginia sun. Every chance I had, I waited under a tree, to get some relief from the blazing sun.** In the Virginia summer, this kind of heat is considered normal.

In the Niagara Peninsula, this would have been a heat wave! But Tedd took it all in stride. After the 9 holes, I was ready to quit. **But Tedd said, "Dad, do you mind waiting in the van while I do a few more holes?"**

Here he was, the cancer patient who one year earlier could not last more than an hour or so shopping at Best Buy, eager to play 2 more holes in the hot Virginia sun! I was very encouraged. What an improvement! **We all felt sure that we had seen an end to the dreaded cancer. It was gone, never to return again. Or so we believed.**

Ellen and I returned home after a great visit encouraged to believe that everything was all right. Their lives were on track and I had only one more year to teach! I loved teaching. But after almost 34 years, I welcomed the idea of following my own interests. We would be able to visit next year any time we wanted!

CHARLES G. PEDLEY

8 *The End of New Beginnings*

Tedd did not see his nephew, born a few days after they left for Virginia, until Canadian Thanksgiving, the first Monday in October. Again the saints at Shiloh were very understanding and allowed Tedd and Rebecca to visit their family as we all met back in Attleboro, Massachusetts. They had great news for us.

Originally, Shiloh had only five or six youth in attendance. There was not much that such a small number could do. But in the few short months that Tedd and Rebecca had been there the attendance had mushroomed to about 30! What a happy time for a couple that could have been separated by death over two years earlier! And happy for us as well. I think parents are happiest when their children are doing well!

Since I was still teaching, we did not see Tedd and Rebecca again until Christmas. Ann and Jon with their new baby could not travel very easily, so it was the easiest plan for all of us to meet again in

Attleboro. Tedd had the flu, but with Becca's help had driven the 500 mile trip to be with the family.

He seemed to recover somewhat after a few days, but we all had an unspoken, uneasy feeling that maybe, just maybe the dreaded cancer was returning again! We cast those terrible thoughts out of our minds and enjoyed the family times with Nathanael the new grandson, his first Christmas! Not that he would remember any of it!

We all returned home hoping to hear in a few weeks that Tedd was fine! That news was not to be.

Instead he was getting worse. They sought out a local doctor who could refer them to a good cancer doctor. It did not take long to discover that it was back! **The problem was that since Tedd's bone marrow was so young, not much could be done. It was like a new-born baby's but without the natural immunity.**

I remember vividly back to our time in Detroit. Tedd's first prognosis was an 85% chance of survival, then the next time, 45%, then with the bone marrow, 25%, and then when the lumps were still there but not active, 10 or 15%. Finally the doctors said they would like to try one more time with a drug that had been used before with promising results.

But Tedd and Becca, looking at the results of chemotherapy and the bone marrow transplant were not too sure. Every time it came back his chances of survival had been reduced. Finally with only a 10 or 15% chance, they went home to pray about what to do.

They both came to the same conclusion, independently. They had the privilege of having one of the best cancer doctors in the United States, one with an enviable record of fighting cancer successfully, but each time Tedd's chances of surviving were smaller. They felt there was only one choice. If Tedd endured chemotherapy again with its terrible taste of metal in the mouth, with his hair falling out, with days in the hospital on intravenous, with possible mouth sores and nausea, if he then died anyway, it would be a horrible way to spend the last few days of his life! And the prognosis was not getting more hopeful, but less!

They felt there was one choice but wanted the reassurance of their Detroit pastor-mentors and their family. They told us their feelings. After praying, we all agreed. It was their decision, but my wife knowing a little about how bad chemo makes you feel, perhaps agreed the most. *We couldn't picture a worse scenario than feeling sick for months, drugs, no hair, terrible tastes, eating even though nothing tastes good, feeling sick to the stomach, and having no energy to do anything but rest.*

Perhaps it was time to combine good health food and faith in their creator. **The best that man had to offer had been done and nothing worked!** Even though he recovered each time and had been getting stronger, here we were again faced with the awful disease. Now it was time to rely on the one who, for some reason known only to Him, had allowed this unrelenting sickness to return.

After his bone marrow treatment in 1996 and for all of 1997, **Tedd had every sign of being healed. He felt better and stronger every week. He was given a chance to fulfill his lifelong dream of becoming a pastor, with gratifying results.** The kids and adults of Shiloh loved this young couple more than any other group on earth could. They took Tedd on knowing that **he had not been declared well**, having the faith that if he got sick, why couldn't they pray as well as any group and see God's hand? Doesn't the Bible say,

"Jesus Christ the same yesterday and today and forever?"

I hesitate to go into the rest of the details. If you have ever had the experience of knowing a loved one with terminal cancer you probably know all too well. And yet they say about 80% of all cancers found early are curable. My wife survived! My mother-in-law survived. Many that I know had lived. But why was Tedd getting worse? **We still had great faith that God would at the last minute reach down His loving hand and perform a miracle that man had not yet been able to do.**

Several times in praying for Tedd, I said to God, knowing full well that God does not make these kind of bargains, ***"God, I have lived a good life, but Tedd is so young, only 26. He has so much life to live and such promise! Please let me die and let him live! He can help so many people understand your kingdom. My time has passed. Please God!"***

But here I am writing these words, hoping to encourage many who read them. **When does the encouragement start?** Keep reading and you will see the miracle that God performed. Not the miracle we expected or asked for but still a miracle nonetheless!

9 *Rebecca the Strong*

They got the news from the doctor. Because his bone marrow was so young, it would have killed him to do any more chemotherapy. Two choices - either let the cancer fluids build up in his body until it put so much pressure on his heart and lungs that he couldn't breathe or his heart could not pump - or radiation to attempt to kill some of the more serious tumors. This would NOT heal the disease but simply make his time more comfortable.

Not much of a choice. Radiation it had to be. Every day, Tedd had to be dressed, put in the wheelchair, and then lifted into the car. That is easy to say, but it was hard to do. Volunteers from the church helped drive since Becca needed to wheel Tedd into the treatment centre while someone else was parking the car. Despite her small build, somehow or other she helped what was left of Tedd in and out of his wheelchair, even lifting him up so that he could have a 'donut' underneath him to relieve the sores due to the constant sitting in the recliner, day and night.

When we were able to go down and be with them, we took our turn driving the one hour trip to the hospital in Richmond.

Tedd slept most of the way. Occasionally he lifted his head to look toward me and say, "Dad, music?" I would put one of his favourite worship CD's in the player and adjust the sound for him. He would simply give me the thumbs up to indicate that the level was okay. It was very hard for him to talk in spite of the oxygen tanks that had to go everywhere with him.

Early in June, the doctor turned to my daughter and Pastor Mike, "***Well, it looks like this will be all wrapped up by July 4.***" ***They looked at the doctor, trying to sort out what he was saying. The expression on his face told the story.*** This meant one thing - Tedd was about one month from death.

We got the news by phone.

Now my memories were all flooding back. I had been sitting in church, my mind wandering. I had to ask, "***God, how do I pray for Tedd this time?*** Do I pray for grace to go through the ordeal or do I pray for his healing?" In my mind I distinctly heard the words, "***Joyful Mourning***". It was like they were placed in my mind as an answer to my prayer. "But God, how can this be? Why had so many little miracles occurred only to have Tedd die anyway?

Why had his heart started again when they were operating to make a port to relieve the pressure of the fluid build-up around his heart? Why had he recovered twice from intense chemotherapy and from the bone marrow treatment? Why did the CAT scan both times find no trace of the disease only to have it return in November? Why didn't he just die over 3 years ago when he first got the disease? Why, when so many serious cancer patients die about one year after diagnosis, did Tedd keep recovering?" **Surely God must have a better plan.**

For some reason, I wrote the words "***Joyful Mourning***" on the top of the page in my open Bible, right above Psalm 1. I guess the pastor must have been preaching from this book. I do not know. I cannot remember. I was having a talk with God. But I could not believe that I had heard correctly so I got angry at Satan for this foul disease that was taking my son-in-law from us. I asked God for healing again. God had answered that prayer at least twice before, why not one more time?

I should have listened to the words that were implanted in my mind. Perhaps in some small way, I wondered if God was preparing me for the end, but I could not believe it at the time.

I finished up my report cards. An early retirement plan was allowing me to retire at the end of May that year instead of June. Then we were Virginia-bound.

My wife and I had learned to just enjoy the trip. We gladly took in the sights, the sounds, the Pennsylvania countryside, the beautiful hills and valleys with tiny farms dotting the landscape connected by ribbons of roads. And then finally, Virginia, the place we had learned to love with its scenic country highways wandering through the lush countryside with beautiful farms, mountain views, and shining streams rushing from the mountains and underneath the highways.

My wife loves photography. Every once in a while she would see something that she absolutely had to take a picture of. She photographed a farm, an estate with red-brick posts bearing its name, a gate, the winding drive up to a magnificent house, horses grazing in the surrounding fields and the Blue Ridge

Mountains as a backdrop. They make puzzles and postcards out of scenes like these!

The 10 hour drive could extend to 15 hours if the traffic did not cooperate. But for the first time, I started to have doubts about Tedd living. It would hit me and the tears would start streaming down my cheeks. I would look at my wife and say, "I don't want Tedd to die."

In the Bible Jesus had raised Lazarus from the dead. I have heard missionary stories from around the present-day world of others being raised from the dead. God is all-powerful. He had created the universe and this small world. Why would He not just lift His little finger and make Tedd better? ***"Why not one more Lazarus, Lord?"***

We would both have a good cry and then it would be okay. Whatever happened, we would be able to face it. But we would not stop praying. Maybe, just maybe, he would still live.

For the last few months, Tedd required so much care, not being able to do anything for himself that the church had arranged teams of volunteers, two at a time to come in and spend the night from 11 PM to 6 or 7 AM each morning. This allowed Becca to get some sleep so she could attend to him during the day.

When I took my turn, Tedd would often motion that he wanted his legs and feet rubbed. Even though his face made him look like '90 pounds soaking wet', his legs and feet had swollen up at least twice the normal size. Since Hodgkin's attacks the lymph system, these fluids were not draining out properly. It made his legs became painful and itchy and the only relief he could get was when we massaged them. By this time, he had morphine for the pain and other drugs to relieve the various symptoms that were part of the disease.

It seemed like every five minutes Tedd would stir and need something; water, pills, rubbing, bathroom trips. It was my privilege to help serve this young man of God.

Have you ever said something so stupid that you wish you could take it back?

One day when my wife took my daughter out for the day to Richmond, I volunteered to look after Tedd. When they returned, I blurted out something that still occasionally haunts me to this day, "Tedd worked my fingers to the bone!" And then realizing how terrible that complaint must have seemed to Tedd, who could do nothing for himself, I quickly added, "But I would do it all again!" How careless that remark had been. I would have to forgive myself over and over again for speaking so carelessly.

My wife and I had to return home to make the final arrangements for my pension.

On July 20 at about 11 PM, the phone rang. My daughter was very upbeat. She was an optimistic person but this time she sounded unusually hopeful. The doctor had seen a remarked improvement. Tedd had even been able to lie down on the couch for the first time in months! Was this the beginning of the expected miracle? After a few moments, she said she had to go. Pastor Mike was calling for her. Tedd needed her.

At 2:45 AM the next morning I found out Tedd would never need her again. Pastor Mike had called her because Tedd had just taken his last quick breathes and died peacefully next to the Pastor who treated him like a son. He had died when I was on the phone with Becca. They waited and silently prayed. Was Tedd to be raised like Lazarus? The hope was there, but it was not to be.

Becca told me later that it was like heaven had opened up and not only allowed Tedd to pass in but some of the beauty, the calm, and the peace of heaven to descend into the room. There was a feeling, not of sorrow but awe, a cloud of peace and joy descending from heaven. She said at that moment, if she could have taken Tedd back, she would not have. How could she deprive him of that glorious feeling that he would experience **for all eternity**. No pain, no oxygen, no more crises, no more pills, no swollen feet, no painful punctures to drain fluid from around his lungs.

We packed and made all the arrangements to look after our cat and my home business. By 6:00 AM we were on the road.

Because his parents had to come all the way from Washington state, the funeral was delayed for five days. Friday night was to be a celebration of his life. His friends from the church, other pastors that knew him, friends from as far away as New Jersey, New York and Michigan, his family, my daughter Ann and husband Jon came to pay tribute to this life. A short but meaningful one. Oh how I wish I had video-taped the wonderful praise that was heaped on my son-in-law. But it is locked forever in the vault of my mind.

On Saturday, the graveside service was short. Everything that needed to be said had already been spoken.

I admired my daughter's strength many times, but here she was, a widow at 25 years old, asking that the elders of the church gather around and pray for the youth. Tedd, in those few short months, had planted in them seeds of service to God and to their fellow man. He would not be around to water them and harvest the fruit. Others would have to do that. We needed to pray that those seeds would not die but flourish, that Tedd's ministry to them would not be in vain.

Even though I felt the loss of my son-in-law, I was so proud of my daughter. Instead of thinking of her loss, she was thinking of the teens who had just lost their much-loved youth pastor. Through almost four years of marriage and sickness, through happy times and many hard ones, she had remained strong.

Looking back, even though Tedd had great faith for God's healing of his body, towards the end, I remember him giving little clues which showed that he knew he was dying.

He motioned to me to come close to the recliner and told me, "Dad, I told God, that if he is going to take me to take me quickly." A few months later, Becca found on the computer a journal entry that Tedd had written. "*I am dying.*" it said. He knew.

And yet right to the end, he maintained his sense of humour. I remember when he would look up and whisper, "Dad?" to get my attention. Then he motioned for me to come to him. I thought he needed help doing something or other. Then he said, holding up two fingers, "Hold my fingers." As I went to reach out to grasp his fingers, he would suddenly pull them away and slap them on my hand and say, "**Tag. You're it**!"

Now what? Would my daughter come home and start again with her life? Would she go and live with her sister Ann in Massachusetts? No she could not bear to leave the youth that had prayed so hard, loved Tedd so much, and lost him, to lose her too! She had to stay. Even though there would be many changes, she had to stay.

Of course she had to move out of the house where she and Tedd had lived for almost exactly one year. Six months of joy and six months of sadness and hope.

She was invited to move in with the Turneys. Bob was one of the elders and his wife Alice, a nurse. Their family was grown up and they had an extra bedroom. Other friends in the church stored Rebecca's furniture. She would become like a daughter to them. Alice and Bob loved her as if she were their own. They refused to take any money for food or board. When she offered, Bob said, "Get those medical bills paid, Rebecca, then we'll see."

When the medical bills were all paid, months later, she offered again and Bob said, "That car out there is getting older. It is going to have to be replaced soon. Save your money for another car."

Even though we made frequent visits every month or two to encourage Rebecca and let her talk as you can only talk to your own family, we could not have asked for a better place for her to stay. In the church was another couple, old enough as well to be Becca's parents, who also treated her like a daughter.

Whenever she needed to talk, the Boggs were there if the Turneys were busy.

Linda and Mike had two sons, no daughters. I think Linda loved Rebecca like the daughter she never had, much like the way I loved Tedd.

Because Tedd had set up a youth staff, Rebecca was able to continue and take his place as youth pastor for several months with their help. The generous church gave her three months of salary with no strings attached. She could have done as she wanted. But she could not leave the youth, just yet. They needed help to go through the loss of their youth pastor. She had to be there for them.

By the end of October she was offered a job in the Virginia Central Bank in Cumberland C.H. Working full-time and doing youth ministry began to take a toll on her life. She was always running to and from work, planning youth ministry, and going to meetings. She realized she could not keep this up indefinitely. She informed the elders and the youth staff that starting in the new year she would be happy to help but could not continue to lead. They understood. Tedd had done this full-time. She was working and trying to carry on the ministry as well.

JOYFUL MOURNING

Rebecca, who had never had any problems attracting male friends, decided this time, it would be different. To honour her husband and God she prayed and said, "God, how long should I wait before I consider getting on with my life?" She had the impression that eight months would be suitable. And now I will tell you the encouraging part. About time, right?

CHARLES G. PEDLEY

10 The Miracle

Though it was Rebecca's wish to marry again, by the spring of 1999, she still felt no assurance from the Lord that she would be married again. She was committed to not demand God give her a husband, even if it meant being alone the rest of her life. One sunny afternoon, she felt God calling her to take a drive, and thought she heard Him telling her that he had a surprise for her if only she would obey.

She got in her car and drove the winding Virginia roads until she ended up on the steps of a pretty, white church. As she rested there, gazing across the field, she heard the Lord say, **"He's there waiting. Her eyes filled with tears, as she realized what this meant. God indeed had someone for her! She even thought she saw a glimpse of her future husband! She saw a young man, sitting on the steps of a big house, playing the guitar. She felt that he would be older than her, and ready to take care of all of her needs. She felt he would be in the ministry also, and that she would be able to**

come alongside of him and help him. And she felt he would have a love and gift for music, as she did.

Rebecca from age 5 had often sung in school talent shows and done an amazing job for one so young. Later she and Ann were asked several times to sing together in our own and other churches. She had taken piano lessons in high school. And *it just happened* that one of her electives at Bible college, had been taking individual voice lessons from a lady trained to sing opera! It is there Rebecca learned that even with a fine voice, it requires all of you to sing with strength.

In the pile of sympathy cards, there was one from a young pastor in Arcade, New York. But knowing that it was not God's timing, she did not write back.

In the summer of 1999, she visited her sister, Ann and husband Jon. When Jon discovered that Scott Laird had written her a letter, he strongly encouraged her to write back to him. Anticipation grew in her heart as she discovered that this friend of the family matched the description of the man she felt the Lord had promised her!

So in August of 1999, Rebecca went back home to Virginia determined to write back to Scott and she did.

At about the same time Pastor Scott, who was now 34, had set apart three days to fast and pray. Three days later, he received the letter from Rebecca. This timing felt significant, especially since he had asked the Lord about his single status earlier in the year and had been surprised to clearly hear the answer, **"I am doing a quick work. You will be amazed."** With these words, Scott had felt God impress on his heart that He did have someone for him and that he would meet her in the fall of that year..

Scott remembered that he had met Rebecca at Jon, his Bible college friend's wedding to our daughter, Ann, ten years before, but he could not remember what she looked like. However as they began a correspondence by mail, it quickly became clear that they were meant for each other. I think the U.S. postal service had to put on extra trucks to carry the volume of letters that started to flow north and south between Arcade NY and Cartersville, Virginia. Eventually I think the phone lines started to heat up as minutes, then hours were spent on the phone getting to know each other.

In October of 1999, Rebecca was coming home to spend Canadian Thanksgiving with us and Scott wrote immediately asking if he could see her since she was coming north. Her mother, asked her, *"What if you don't like the way he looks?"* She said, "I already love him!" God had placed this love in her heart all those months before.

Pastor Scott picked her up at the airport and brought her to our home in beautiful Fonthill. Within two days, they felt like they had known each other for years.

The plan proceeded, engagement and then wedding plans were made and in August 2000, just one year after her first letter was sent, Rebecca Woodworth married Pastor Scott Charles Laird.

They are happily married and living about an hour and a half south of Fonthill, in ski country, near Arcade New York. Their first-born son Ian James was born on my 58th birthday - **November 18th. To top it all off, this day in 2001 was also my wife's mother, Great Grandma Noake's 80th birthday, and Ian** *came just in time so that we could meet him and still drive back to Canada for her party!*

It was like a gift from God, because as you remember, every November became a trial as Tedd fell sick again. Now God had given us a "***redeemed" November***. No longer would we think of Tedd being sick but of Ian being born!

As of 2004, Rebecca and Scott had their second son, Macgregor. A third son Nathan pleasantly surprised them in October of 2008.

Oh and by the way, Pastor Scott does indeed play the guitar and writes music as well. He helped my daughter record her first CD. [2]

Now if you still think that God can't put you together with your future mate and you have to do it all, look under every rock and search in every hollow tree for someone to spend the rest of your life with, THINK AGAIN!

You have just read a miracle of God putting a couple together. He can and will perform miracles or God-incidences in your life if you trust him and put Him first in your life!

---

[2] **Broken Clay** by Rebecca Woodworth Laird is released by Laird Studios

We can always decide to do 'it our way' as the song says or we CAN do it GOD'S way. Psalm 139 comes to mind.

11 My Way or The Highway?

Psalm 139

13. For you formed my inmost being. You knit me together in my mother's womb.

14. I will give thanks to you, For I am fearfully and wonderfully made. **Your works are wonderful. My soul knows that very well.**

15. My frame wasn't hidden from you, When I was made in secret, woven together in the depths of the earth. [cp- word for "earth" also means "womb"]

16. Your eyes saw my body. In your book they were all written, The days that were ordained for me, When as yet there were none of them.[3]

Did you just read those words? Or did you skip them to hear the rest of the story? If you DID NOT READ THEM, please GO BACK and read them now.

There are really several ways to go here. If you do not believe in God, then you probably would not

---
[3] Ps. 139: 13-16

have read this far, but if you have and you don't believe in God, then I will soon share with you the most AMAZING "COINCIDENCE"! *I call them God-incidents!* However for those of you who believe there is a superior intelligence to your own, I will explain something I am learning.

It is not the purpose of this book to explain why you must be an ostrich with your head buried in the sand if you don't believe in God or the Bible. There are hundreds if not thousands of evidences which point to a supreme being who started everything that you see around you. The stars, the sun, the beautiful scenery on earth, the glory of the heavens on a dark clear night, the motions of the earth around the sun, life itself all point to a creator! As a former science teacher, I cannot resist giving you one evidence.

Do you know that the earth is traveling at exactly the right speed to sustain life? If the earth were to speed up in its orbit around the sun, it would fling itself out into space like a rock tied to a string which is swung around above the head, faster and faster, until the outward pressure makes you stop the swinging or the string leaves your hand. Or how about the outward pressure as you travel around a bend on a highway at a speed a little bit too fast? You feel the car leaning to the outside of the turn and if you went even faster than you could control, the car would eventually try to go straight off the road.

And if the earth went just a little slower, it would not be long before the force of gravity from the sun would pull it into a death spiral, around and around, ever closer until it was pulled into the sun. Neither of these actions would support life. If we left our orbit we would get farther and farther from the sun and colder and colder until life would cease to exist. Surely I do not have to explain what crashing into the sun would mean?

Now, let's look at that Psalm! It points out several things about God that you may wonder about if you are grieving.

"His works are wonderful."

What is so wonderful to be 25 years old and lose your husband?

"My soul knows that very well."

It tells us that our days were "ordained" for us **BEFORE we WERE BORN,** "...when as yet there were none of them". He was involved in your life, whether you realized it or not, BEFORE YOU WERE CREATED!

No matter what you believe about the Bible, there are ONLY TWO CHOICES!

1. You AGREE with these verses or
2. You DISAGREE with these verses!

What does "ordained" mean? It means 'purposed, scheduled, put into order, approved of, allowed the happening'.

This Psalm seems to be telling us that whatever happens, God **saw it** before we were even born and **allowed it to be**. He said it was **okay**.

How can it be **okay** for a young married lady of 25 to lose her husband, her lover, her life and have to start all over again? Does that not seem cruel and heartless?

*But if there is a God, he certainly **knows more** than we do! What is the most complicated thing you have ever created? Have you ever created even one living thing? God has created the universe, many galaxies, the countless stars of the Milky Way and all life on earth from the simplest one-celled amoeba to human beings. He put everything we needed to live* *and survive for generations on this "spaceship", called earth.*

We value human life and well we should. When we get up in the morning and start to contact other people we see **bodies** with clothes on. We do **not see** what God values even more than our bodies, our SOUL, and our SPIRIT. Oh, we detect those parts of people before long, but they **are not** evident to our senses. We have to hang around someone for a while to really see their soul and spirit.

The soul is made up of your MIND, your WILL, and your EMOTIONS.

Your spirit is that part of you that makes you, **you**! That part of you that makes you different than all other living creatures on earth!

But the Bible tells us that man looks on the outward appearance of people but **God looks on the heart.** He looks beyond our outward appearance and looks at what is in our soul and spirit. He cares more about what is inside you than what is outside. He **cares about your character** more than your body.

As people, we value the bodies of others, at least most of us do. **But God values the attitudes and values INSIDE of YOU that others may not** *always see, especially if they only have a casual acquaintance with you.*

So to be blunt, if your body dies, **God cares**, but He **values more** what happens to your **soul** and **spirit**. If your soul and spirit die, you may still have a body but you would be dead inside! Have you ever patiently broken open a precious pecan, only to find it rotten on the inside? What a letdown! God cares about YOU more than most of us do! **He wants our bodies to live! But EVEN MORE, HE WANTS OUR SOUL AND SPIRIT TO LIVE! He is not impressed by hollow, rotten nuts!**

It is difficult to explain, but God will allow things to happen to our body that may not be very pleasant. Why? Because then our **soul** and **spirit** can grow! Remember the verse from Rebecca's song?

"Lovingly He sees your tiny hand

And dreams of all the plans He has for you

Tenderly, His finger

Has molded the inner parts of you

And as each part He created

A smile on His face, a tear in His eye"

God knew from before your birth that 'bad things' will happen to you. They happen to everyone! And He sheds a tear because He must allow these hard things to happen or put us all on strings so that we are puppets! But **He knows** that YOU CAN OVERCOME "bad things" with GOOD ATTITUDES and learn valuable lessons which can help others going through hard times. It is all in the attitude!

Am I saying that when someone dies, we should just cast it off casually and say, "*Oh well, it is all for my good*" and never feel sorry for the loss? Of course not! **You MUST GRIEVE**. If you do not, all those EMOTIONS will be bottled up inside you until you burst like a pimple! Your emotions, your feelings, your thoughts need to be released or you will gradually die inside! On the inside where God sees who you really are, you will become hard like a rock, bitter not better. You have met people like that haven't you? People who seem so hard that if they fell, they would crack! Let all those feelings out. In fact God LOVES YOU EVEN MORE when you are honest with Him about your feelings. He knows how you feel anyway. You can't hide it. So let it out! **What kind of** *a friend would He be if He couldn't take your anger and your hurt and still LOVE YOU?*

What I am saying, is that we need to come to the conclusion that King David in the Bible did. **We all need to agree with God, that our days are ordained. They may not feel good all the time. They may feel awful, but God said, "I trust you to learn from this and become stronger!"**

I hope I have helped you to understand in some small way why God allows these 'tragic' things to come into our lives and KNOWS that we CAN MOVE BEYOND them and be stronger because of them.

Up to now, I have painted my daughter as someone who was so strong, she didn't even shed a tear. I believe God gave her a supernatural strength for the moment. I was even a little worried at the time, when I felt sadder than she appeared to be.

The tears came. Apparently in buckets! Ever the thoughtful man, Pastor Mike made sure one of the ladies was at the house with her as she tried to pack up. Oh how I wish I had insisted on staying to help her, to be there for her as her "daddy" again. She said she wanted to do this by herself. We respected her wishes. However, Pastor Mike said that over the next few weeks as she went back to the house, some days not much was accomplished except grieving for the loss of Tedd. **Everything she looked at reminded her of little things they had shared together**. Joyful and sad moments, but shared with love.

And now may I share some things about grieving?

CHARLES G. PEDLEY

12 Grieving Your Loss

A curious thing occurred in the two years before my daughter got remarried. Tedd helped her to grieve his loss! **What?** He was dead. How could he help?

As my daughter was sorting and packing up the house where she and Tedd had lived, she came across a set of notes. The notes were ones that Tedd had taken in a **class on grieving** at Elim Bible Institute. **The other God-incident was that the class was given by a professor who had lost his wife. As a result of his loss, he decided to study the process of grieving so he would understand what he was going through.**

He realized how important this understanding was and started the grieving class to teach young pastors and Christian workers what he had learned. **She kept these notes under her bed and read through part of them each night in order to understand what she was going through. It must have been a mixture of pain and pleasure as she looked at the printed pages with the blanks filled in with Tedd's handwriting!**

Mourning does strange things to all of us. Sometimes when we talk to someone in mourning, we do not know what to say. Previously, I have always avoided bringing up a dead spouse's name thinking that this would to be too hard for the person to handle. In studying the process, this is one of the myths that is hard to break. As the professor pointed out in his notes, he could not understand why people NEVER mentioned his wife's name. He still loved her! Had they forgotten her already? Didn't they care about her at all?

Of course these friends of his were just trying to be considerate, trying hard not to bring up painful memories. But without meaning to, they were actually increasing the pain. **Most people want and need to talk about their loss. It is therapeutic.** But in our attempts to be considerate of someone who has experienced a loss, we can actually be increasing their pain and perhaps slowing down the grieving process.

We also find it difficult to know what to say to someone who is mourning. I have never felt comfortable saying the trite little words that we all say, but what else do you do? Sometimes if we are not thoughtful before we speak, we may blurt out something really stupid.

One example of this would be what happened to Rebecca several months after Tedd had passed away. She was working in the bank and in walked a mother with her daughter who had been part of their youth group. Rebecca remarked on the fact that she had not seen her daughter at youth group for a long time. The lady said to her, "**You just don't know what it's like to lose your youth pastor!**" Rebecca said, "No, I don't." But she felt inside like screaming out, "*He was my HUSBAND! I think I know better than you what loss is!*" However she realized the lady was just being honest, not trying to be offensive at all.

A few months after Rebecca married Scott, she fell into depression. This did not make any sense to her at all! Here she was, her life moving on again, married to a very thoughtful and considerate man, being depressed. After a while Scott thought it wouldn't hurt for her to see a Christian counsellor. They sought out recommendations and found one. Rebecca went for a few sessions and the counsellor said, "**Rebecca, I think that because of what you**

went through, you started to believe a lie. I think we should have a session on 'inner healing'."

Now for those of you who have red flags in front of your eyes, ***inner healing*** means just what it says, "INNER HEALING". No strange incantations or reciting of magic words. We are not afraid, for the most part, of OUTER HEALING, healing of the body through a doctor's care. But what is ***even more important***, is what is inside of us! Our soul, our spirit. The two strangers that live inside us.

The counsellor helped Rebecca to discover the time when she had started to believe the lie. She had seen that Rebecca had started thinking that yes, God would let her serve Him, but that her life was never going to be easy!

She asked Rebecca to remember those moments when she was looking after Tedd, the pain that she felt inside, not only for Tedd but for what she was going through. ***She had repressed her pain***, realizing that Tedd had so much more need than she did, that her needs were not important! The counsellor reminded her that we all have needs, whether we are sick or not and Jesus cares about all of us equally.

Because someone is sick and is needier does NOT MEAN that our needs are unimportant!

The counsellor had Rebecca picture the worst memories of trying to help Tedd and the moment when she started to believe the lie. **Then she asked Rebecca to picture Jesus standing there, unable to help, with tears in His eyes. He went through each moment of pain with her. He was there!** With this help, Rebecca was able to discover the lie that she had started to believe and start over again. She realized again that God loved her and wanted the best for her and yes, He would actually allow her to be happy again.

Depression is a strange thing and it can be hard to pin down the cause. The causes can be physical, emotional, attitudinal or spiritual. But with a good counsellor Rebecca was able to get back on track and become the happy, bubbly, young lady again.

The wonderful thing about this true story is that I shared it with a friend who was going through bouts of depression. He suddenly said, *"I never thought of that before! Jesus is going through this with me!"* And the even better news is that his bouts of depression ended and he is on track again! This revelation from God broke the hold of depression on him. **The Bible says that if we know the truth, the truth will set us free!** I believe he was set free. Every once in a while he reminds me that even though he occasionally still gets depressed, that moment was the one that things started to change .

You might wonder if He was there when you were going through a difficult time, "Why didn't He do something?" There is no instant answer. Sometimes He does! But being God, the Father, sometimes, He doesn't! He is sovereign. If every time, a 'bad' thing happened, He stepped in, we would be deprived of free will. Just like our children. Are we *never* going to let them stand up and try to walk because they may hurt themselves? Are we *never* going to let them ride a bike because they may fall and get hurt? If we did, they would always remain babies, never learning or growing.

I am NOT a counsellor, a psychologist, or a psychiatrist.[4] I am not going to pretend I know exactly how to help you. **But what I do know is that God loves you and has loved you since before you**

---

[4] My majors in university were psychology, counselling and Christian counselling.

were in your mother's womb. He has a plan for your life. He wants you to be fulfilled and alive! He would like to use you to help the many hurting people in this world of ours. Will He take away all our pain? Not with a snap of the finger but if you allow yourself to be open and ask for His help and if necessary the help of a good counsellor, you too can get back on track again.

Do not expect to be healed instantly. If you are, more power to you but it is not the norm. Whatever you do, do not shut up your pain, locking it away somewhere in your brain and try to forget it.

You cannot forget it. Scientists discovered many years ago that everything we have experienced is still there in our brains. Normally we may not have the key to open up those memories. But they are there! Our body senses experienced them.

A famous neurosurgeon and scientist, Dr. Wilder Penfield, touched various parts of a person's brain when under local anaesthesia and asked the person to report what they were remembering. One individual reported that he was remembering waking up in the morning to the smell of bacon frying and was experiencing all the senses that he did at the original time. It is something that he had forgotten all about but as Dr. Penfield touched various parts of his brain, these memories all came flooding back like he was living this moment in life all over again.

If you attempt to lock these feelings away, which is not natural, they will resurface in anger, hostility, and grouchiness or in some physical way such as stomach ulcers. They may resurface like a pimple bursting and spewing its pussy contents all over everyone nearby! Of course I do not mean physically but emotionally.

Let me explain the concept of **body, soul** and **spirit**.

13 Body, "Meet Soul and Spirit"

A little background information is necessary to explain this concept which books have been written about. I will try to be brief.

We know each other as bodies to begin with. Our **bodies** are the visible containers that hold our emotions and spirits. But as we get to know someone our first impressions of them may change as we start to see their personalities.

One example of this is related to one of our former associate pastors, Pastor Stan. Pastor Stan is a good-looking man with dark brown hair and has a great singing voice! He was a youth pastor living in Newfoundland with his wife (who came from our church). When he would come home to visit, he would usually be asked to sing a solo. Rebecca said that he has the nicest singing voice of anyone she has ever heard. He never said much, just got up and sang. I had the impression that he was '*stuck up*'. He just got up and sang and without looking at anyone, would go back to his seat.

For some reason, I interpreted this behaviour as being 'stuck' on himself. Oh, I never said anything, except maybe to my wife. It was just an impression. But then the day came when Stan and his family moved to Welland and became one of our pastors. I got to know him as I helped him with his computer.

He was so thoughtful that I don't think he really told me how he felt about the computer. It was one of those notebooks where you have to switch the floppy and CD drives. It had been purchased by the church from my business, *Computerworks*. He would mention that it was a little inconvenient but right away talk about how much he loved its other characteristics such as the clear screen. So, it seemed to be something he could live with. Little did I know until after the warranty was gone, that he would have liked to trade it for one that had everything self-contained.

He was so thoughtful of my feelings that I do not believe he told me how he really felt. This man with a nature very sensitive to the feelings of others was definitely NOT the same man I had pictured when I only knew him as a body! **I had totally misread his inner self.** What I read as stuck-up was just a slight natural shyness or self-consciousness.

So you see, what we see is NOT ALWAYS WHAT WE GET!

Let me explain the concept of soul and spirit. Your soul consists of your mind, your will and your emotions. Your spirit consists of that part of you that is open to God or to satanic (negative) influence.

You have a brain. You may be anywhere from very smart to just average. You may be capable of being a doctor or a nuclear scientist or maybe a gas station attendant or clerk. Our minds have different capabilities when it comes to absorbing knowledge. Thank goodness that we are not all the same! Can you imagine a world where everyone wants to be a doctor, lawyer or scientist and we had no clerks, no gas station attendants, no mechanics, no garbage collectors, and no city workers to fix our streets? Our civilization would come to a standstill! Thank goodness we all have different capabilities due to our different minds!

You have a will. Sometimes when we get stubborn we should call it a 'WON'T'. You decide whether to do something or not. You always have a choice! This applies to grieving as well. *It is okay to hurt, to feel your loss, even to be angry for*

moments at the creator, as long as you realize in the long run that getting angry at God only does you harm. He is our Father. When we are parents, we do things we cannot always explain to our children. Their little minds could not understand it until they get older and more mature. God cannot always explain to us why He allows pain and hurt. That does not mean He doesn't care. ***Remember Rebecca's song? Remember Psalm 139?*** He was there when you were formed in your mother's womb and He has a plan for your life!

And that brings us to our emotions, our feelings. We feel love, hate, disgust, sadness, compassion, and anger; a whole gamut of emotions. If we always acted outwardly according to how we feel inwardly at the moment, there would be a lot more murders!

Then, there is our spirit. It is a little unseen part of you that allows you to be open to God the creator or Satan, the 'uncreator', the destroyer, the accuser, the father of lies. At some time in your life you decided to either believe God or believe Satan. You either chose to follow a path of 'good' or a path where you let your feelings control you and act out whatever feeling you happen to have at the time. Mother Theresa or Jeffrey Dahmer. Billy Graham or Sadham Hussein.

Of course, if we have decided to give God control of our spirits, we will not be perfect. We still have to fight against the body and the emotions sometimes. And if we give Satan control, we can still be nice people sometimes. Mobsters are often nice to their families while they secretly kill policemen, bank tellers and enemies of the mob.

Everything we know came to us through our body gates, our eyes, our sense of touch, our hearing, our sense of smell, or taste. If we ate mushed-up liver when we were babies and we did not like the taste, we spit it back out! That is what our daughters did! We thought it would be good for them once in a while. We purchased it mixed with bacon, vegetables or whatever. It did not matter. They were NOT going to eat liver! Their sense of taste told them, "This stuff is terrible! Get it out of here!" So back it came after a few spoonfuls, out the mouth and down the chin!

We always have a choice, but when you are very young you just react to whatever you feel. Have you ever had one of your kids say something embarrassing after looking at someone, "Mom I don't like that man!" We are very embarrassed but they are just reacting in their honest childish way!

As we get older we learn to keep many of our feelings to ourselves. We do this because we realize it is polite AND because gradually we get to know that OUR FEELINGS ARE NOT ALWAYS RIGHT! Remember my reaction to Pastor Stan?

This is all part of the process of growing up. The reason we have powerful computers today is because various people over 100 years ago started to realize that everything can be broken down into two choices. We can always go one way or the other. We can turn the light switch on or off. We can turn right or left. We can get angry every time we feel angry or we can decide that is not a good way to win friends and influence people! Of course, it is not always this simple. Sometimes we may have three choices. Turn right or left or go straight! But there is always the element of choice, unless you always give in to your feelings.

But your feelings may be guided by a damaged spirit. *In order for our spirits to be whole, we have to learn to open them to the creator of life.*

Have you ever bought one of those 'put-it-together-yourself' pieces of furniture? Suppose you opened the box and laid out all the pieces, glanced at the instructions and then said, "I DON'T CARE WHAT THESE INSTRUCTIONS SAY I AM GOING TO PUT THIS THING TOGETHER THE WAY I WANT!!" Wouldn't that be rather foolish? Who knows best how all those pieces fit together? I would think the manufacturer might.

And yet, often we as human beings say exactly the same thing about our lives! I AM NOT GOING TO LISTEN TO THE INSTRUCTIONS! I AM GOING TO LIVE THE WAY I WANT!!" And unfortunately often we do and our lives LOOK LIKE we didn't follow the instructions! ALL MESSED UP! Like a desk with legs protruding from the top and the drawers not fitting properly. Does your life feel this way sometimes? If it does, I respectfully urge you again, get to know the **manufacturer**, God!

Human beings have *never* created life out of dust and never will but I know someone who specializes in it! And you don't even have to dial a 1-800 number to reach Him!

I know right now some of you are saying, "I am not made out of dust!" Why does the Bible say that in Genesis! How ridiculous!"

Is it? What are you made from? Would you say chemicals? What is dust made from? All life on earth consists of atoms and molecules making up chemical compounds that *make us* and *make up dust*!

Trust the owner's manual! It is called the Bible! It is only hard to understand when you don't read it enough.

So you see, God had a plan for us before our birth and still does. *It is the plan which will make us the happiest in life*. Will every day or event be happy? Of course not! But if we ask God to help us and give Him the choice of which way our lives should go, we will be much happier than if we try to build that 'furniture' the way we want to, I mean *our lives* the way we want to!

We were given a body, soul and spirit in the image of God. If we allow God's spirit to control our lives no matter how long or short they are, we will be fulfilled like Tedd was. Were they miserable for four years? No! Did Tedd and Rebecca have worries and fears in those four years? Of course! But they also had ONE who was there when they were formed in their mothers' wombs. One who has always been there, gently trying to let you know He cares when you hurt! One who wants to be with you always until the end of the earth! One who will not leave you nor forsake you!

In case you have not read the introduction, I will repeat here my daughter's song, "**Beautiful**" from her CD, "**Broken Clay**"

Lovingly He sees your tiny hand
And dreams of all the plans He has for you
Tenderly, His finger
Has molded the inner parts of you
And as each part He created
A smile on His face, a tear in His eye
Walking in the smallness of life
Growing in the little things you do
Pressing on although scared and frightened
His gentle hand pulling you through
He was there.
And a lump of clay molded, fitly fashioned
Created in the image of His son
Your heart now beats as one with the Father's
You're made a man, it's done

Beautiful....

From the baby to the man
Oh, beautiful ...
Even though you don't understand
Beautiful
Meet for the Master's use
A lump of clay in His hand
The thoughts that He has planned
You're an instrument in His hand
Beautiful, so beautiful

Beautiful ©*RW Laird*

Did Rebecca feel forsaken by God? Probably many times! But she told her feelings that she was going to believe what God said about her life. Does that mean she didn't hurt or cry? Of course not! She hurt. She cried! We all hurt and cry if we are healthy! **But she knew that somehow or other, God still had a loving plan for her if she was just patient and waited for it. And did He have a plan! You have already seen His plan for the rest of her life!**

Did she know that God had a young man who had also been waiting for God's plan in Arcade, New York? No! But God did! They both waited for God's timing and two years after Tedd died she married the man that God had waiting for her! One who is so thoughtful that when she apologized about having a grieving moment for Tedd, he said, "*Rebecca, you loved him! You can grieve him whenever you need to, I will never feel threatened!*" One who wanted to go down to Virginia and let her Virginia friends meet him so they would know who this man was that was going to take away their Rebecca. One who wanted to go to Tedd's graveside and shed a tear for all that Tedd and Rebecca had gone through. One who would help her complete her CD that she had started with the help of her friends in Virginia. One who thinks of her first before he thinks of himself.

Have you ever wondered if you would ever be happy again? You can be in time by surrendering your feelings to the one who created feelings in us to start with.

I was driving my van, probably on a computer service call, within a year after Tedd's death and I was having a grieving moment, reliving all we had gone through with Tedd and how much we missed him.

I asked God, **"Why did you not just let Tedd die when he first got sick**? Why all the hopes built up so many times only to have him die anyway about four years later? I was not lashing out in anger at God, but just asking Him in honesty. And the distinct answer that came back to me was **"So that you might be found faithful."**

And I knew that this answer was straight from God. **Tears of joy came flooding down my cheeks. I was so happy that God would actually take time out of his busy schedule to answer me**. Tedd's parents were so far away. They could not be there with him. We could and we were. Even though I know that this is only part of the answer, I knew that God was just giving me enough to satisfy my heart's cry at that time.

And He will satisfy yours if you allow Him to! You can pray this prayer if you agree with it.

"God, I don't understand why this has happened to me. I hurt. I feel like I will never truly be normal again. But I thank you for giving me a reason to hope. Thank you for

giving your Son as a sacrifice for my sins and raising Him to life again, defeating death and fear. I resolve to turn from my sins right now and invite You into my life. I am deciding to trust You even if I never understand why I have gone through this crisis. But I pray that You will show me in time how this tragedy in my life can be helpful to others who also are experiencing a loss. In Jesus name, Amen."

We need to understand from a human point of view as well what we are going through. Am I normal? When will I ever get through this? The next chapter explains the process of grieving.

CHARLES G. PEDLEY

14 *The Grieving Process*

This chapter will explain some of the variety of emotions you may feel as you come to grips with your loss.

The Stages of Grieving

These do not occur in a certain order. You may feel like you have passed "that stage" and then feel like you are starting to grieve all over again. Since we are all different, we will all experience mourning in a different way. That having been said, here are the steps.

1. **Denial and Shock** - It may be difficult to accept your loss at first. You may feel that if *only* you had ....*(done this or that)*........., your husband (loved one) would still be alive (or not sick or whatever).

2. **Anger** - You may feel "why me?" You may get angry at your dead or departed spouse (loved one)

and lay blame on them. **My daughter had the weird feeling of anger at Tedd because he died three days before their fourth anniversary.** She felt, "Why couldn't he have waited three more days before he died? At least we could have celebrated our anniversary together!" She realized how silly this was but nevertheless she felt it. If you feel angry at God, tell Him. You won't be the first! Read the Psalms! David seemed to be angry at God many times but in the end always came back to the realization that God's ways are higher than our ways. We cannot always understand why He allows things to happen in life. But we can always agree that **Father knows best**!

3. **Bargaining** - Sometimes people will try to bargain with God and be ready to give up something if only He will return everything to normal. In one way I guess I did this, I said to God, "*God, Tedd is so young and full of zeal. He wants to change the world and make it a better place! I have had a good life! He has only started. Please take me and leave him!*" Of course I realized that this was silly but that is how I felt at the time!

4. **Guilt -** You may feel guilty for things you did or said and blame yourself for your loved one's death or loss. Forgive yourself. No one is perfect. Unless you actually stabbed someone to death or shot them, you are not guilty! Life happens. We will all die sometime. Some, it seems, too soon!

5. **Depression** - You may experience so much loss that you feel like you are walking around in a daze. You may feel numb, even though you are sad and angry underneath. You may feel like lying in bed and staying away from people. ***Usually to get over this, you need the exact opposite***. At least get together with a trusted friend or counsellor and talk about your loss. The depression may leave gradually or something may happen to make you feel happier all of a sudden. Getting together with a person or people who understand will help get rid of the feelings of loneliness over time.

6. **Acceptance -** Gradually, all the other emotions will give way to realizing that life can and will go on. ***You are not the first and will not be the last person to suffer loss!*** You will be able to get rid of things that belonged to your departed mate without feeling totally disloyal. I thought my daughter did this in such a great

way. She took each of Tedd's possessions and thought who might treasure or use them the most. She gave Tedd's Bible to his younger brother who also has a heart to help people understand God the way Tedd did.

7. **Hope** – Yes, there is hope. If you ever lose hope, read the story of how God brought Scott and Rebecca together, again. He does have a purpose for you! And what is more, God takes things that are tragic or 'terrible' and uses them for good. That is what prompted me to write this book over four years after Tedd's death. ***Whenever I had a quiet moment and said to God, "I am almost 60, God. I am healthy. What can I do for you and the rest of humanity? I do not want to waste the time I have left." Every time I prayed this prayer, the feeling came back to me, "Write what you learned!"*** And so I have.

You may experience some or all of these emotions but they will not necessarily occur in the order they are presented. You may feel like you are in a maze not on a road, going back over the same feelings again and again. But they will lessen in time.

If they do not, seek help in a trusted friend, a minister, a counsellor, or a grieving support group.

The next chapter will give you some coping strategies that may make the process a little easier. I emphasize 'a little' because mourning is work. It drains your energy. But it is necessary work and you will come through it!

CHARLES G. PEDLEY

15 *Coping Strategies*

As if it isn't already hard enough when you lose someone you love, you lose more than the person. If you are a wife, you lose your identity. You are no longer a wife.

Rebecca helped Tedd with his youth ministry. When Tedd died, even though she carried on for him for a time, that time ended. Now, suddenly she had no husband to help. No youth ministry. That was who she was. Her husband was gone. Her identity of being connected with Tedd in any way was gone. A new identity had to be forged. It is like growing up all over again!

Often as a couple, you get together with other couples. When your partner is gone, sometimes you get left out because you are not part of a couple anymore. That can make your grieving even more intense. Just when you need to be with people, you get left out. Not only has your husband gone but now your 'couple' friends can be gone too.

It is often very difficult for friends to know how to treat you. It is confusing for them too. Without meaning to be thoughtless, they don't invite you over with other couples because you are not a 'couple' anymore. And besides, maybe it would bring back too many sad memories? What would a party be like if suddenly you broke down crying? It is often easier to just not invite you. So, with no intention of hurting you but perhaps even trying to be thoughtful of how you may feel, you may get hurt again. How many losses can you stand? **Your husband, your identity, your friends? So what is next?**

All of these feelings and events can and unfortunately do happen. How do you get past these hurts? You may think that no one cares but you. Why go on living? **Most people need to have the help of friends, a church family, some support group or maybe even a counsellor, if need be. But there are things you can do yourself. You are not alone. There is one who said He would never leave you nor forsake you. God can become very real to you, perhaps more than ever before if you don't blame Him for your spouse's death and become bitter.**

So what can you do? We are all different. Every strategy listed here may not work for every person. *That is okay! Here is the buffet. Help yourself to whatever works! But do try some of them. You will be nourished! You need to feed your soul and spirit as well as your body.*

1. **Find a friend, a pastor who will allow you to talk when you want to** and not talk when you don't. Rebecca had the Turneys, the family that took her in. Alice and Bob treated her like a daughter. I was so touched when they put Rebecca's name on the slate signpost at the end of their driveway right along with their other children who were away at school. We will always be grateful to them for their wonderful southern hospitality. And when the Turneys were busy, Rebecca could turn to Linda and Mike Boggs, her other '*Virginia parents*'. They were always ready to invite her over, let her mourn, or just gab as the need came. On top of that, they extended their hospitality to us, telling us, that '*our room*' was always ready for us. All we had to do was phone and make sure no one else was using it. And then every month or two, Rebecca needed to talk the way you only can talk to your family. Just to 'let it all out' knowing that they will love you anyway. And we were happy to be there for her. The strange thing is that when that

ended with her marriage to Scott, I felt deprived. I felt like I wasn't necessary to Rebecca anymore! The empty nest syndrome all over again! **We had already experienced the letting go of our daughters, and now we had to let Rebecca go again.** She was an adult. But without realizing it, I guess I enjoyed being needed by her again and it was a little let down when it ended. But in my mind I was glad that her life had been restored. It was in my soul where my feelings live that I felt let down, but happy in my spirit for her.

2. **Don't let anyone tell you to "get on with your life".** That time will come in a year or maybe two. If it goes beyond that, then get professional help. You MUST grieve or the hurt that you feel inside will build up and burst forth in physical symptoms or emotional outbursts or complete despair. You have had a lot of stress. You need time to adjust and mourn your losses. In fact, the letter that Scott wrote to Rebecca right after Tedd's death, said exactly that. He had to grieve some things in his life and he knew. This is the letter that she did not answer until over a year later and was the beginning of their relationship.

3. **Do something you always wanted to do.** Take a trip. Learn to swim. My mother-in-law, Katie Noake, was 58 when she lost her husband. She never had the opportunity to learn how to swim. So, she enrolled in classes for adults and overcame her fear of the water. You won't see her in the Olympics any time soon but she felt good taking steps to overcome this lack in her life. And it made time pass more quickly.

4. **Get some exercise!** I remember a true story I saw on a film that we used to show our elementary students. It was the story of a newspaper reporter who had a bad heart condition. He had had several heart attacks. His heart was in bad shape. At any time, he could have another one. He was very depressed because he did not feel well. He felt like committing suicide but realized that would leave his family with no insurance. So, he thought he would run until his heart gave out. Then no insurance company could say he committed suicide! He ran and ran and ran. Nothing happened except that he started feeling a little bit better. Next day, he did the same thing. He still didn't die. He started feeling so much better about things that he kept running because it made him feel better. He never did have another attack and when he

went back to the doctor the next time, the doctor was amazed how healthy his heart was. Of course that was his physical heart. But exercise can also help a '*broken*' heart.

5. **Allow yourself to talk about your loved one as often as you need to.** Reminisce over photographs and memorabilia preferably with a friend who can be there with you if the waves of grief are too much for you alone. It is all healthy. You may remember your loved one only when they were sick. It was hard remembering the good times with Tedd. We had seen him deteriorate over several months so that he could not do anything for himself, even breathe. For the last several months of his life, he had to be on oxygen. Wherever he went, oxygen tanks were loaded in with him to help him breathe. When he passed away, the freshest memories were of him living in the recliner attached to the oxygen machine 'umbilical cord'. It was difficult to remember the happy times. My wife, being an avid photographer, put together a 'memories' photo album of the good times with Tedd. She did it for his parents who were separated by thousands of miles from their son. But when I saw it I told her I wanted one too. It was my daughter Ann who got the

same photos and made a memory album for me. How wonderful it was to relive the happy experiences which had all but been washed away with the tide of sickness which had overtaken him at the end.

6. **Pray and read the Psalms** for comfort. Psalms 3, 7, 13, 25, 44, 74, 79, 80, Psalms of lament may help.

7. **Eat balanced meals**. Your physical health affects your emotional state.

8. **The first year will be the hardest.** *It will be a year of "firsts" that were shared with your loved one.* The **first birthday** without him, the **first Christmas**, the **first anniversary**. All of these can throw you back into the cycle of grief. That is okay. Just like being a teenager, we all have to go through it.

9. **You may wish to try journaling.** Let me give you an example. Those who know us, know that this was not the first cancer to strike our family. My wife Ellen was diagnosed with lymphoma in 1987. For most of her life she has been a 'journalist'. By that I mean one who journals her experiences. When she was declared well in July 1988, she started to write a book

of her trip through cancer. Since then she has been asked several times to share her experiences with ladies' groups and nurses. Her journal was the source for the encouraging talks which gave others hope. If she had not recorded the good experiences and the bad, her faded memories would not have brought the tears of understanding to many at these meetings who had experienced loss. **You may have already had to bury a loved one; don't bury the memories too!** Research proves that ignoring the loss serves to make you feel even more isolated.

10. **Write a letter to the loved one**. Perhaps there are unresolved feelings that need to be brought out. Rebecca had a weird feeling when Tedd passed away three days before their fourth anniversary. She felt angry that he couldn't even wait for their anniversary to die. Then she felt stupid at having such a terrible thought!

There are many ways of dealing with grief. They will make it more bearable but they will not eliminate it. Nothing can avoid the process any more than one can skip from being a child to being an adult, omitting the sometimes troubling teen years.

But I hope that you have seen there are ways that you can use to help you cope, to help you let out the mourning gradually. **You are not alone! Many have come this way before and survived! In fact, there is one who went through the loss of His Son knowing in advance that it must happen to make a way for the rest of us. That is what happened when Jesus Christ died on the cross!**

If you are Jewish, think of Abraham being willing to sacrifice his only son Isaac because God asked him to. God has promised to never leave us nor forsake us. He was with Rebecca all through the tough times with a sick husband and still there for her after his death. **You can be honest with God and tell Him how you feel but still recognize His right to be God, still recognize that He is sovereign, recognize that He knows more than you will ever know and yet He allowed this loss to come into your life.**

He would only do this for one reason! **He trusts you and knows that you can get through it and learn from it** and be used by Him to help others who are struggling with a similar loss. Who can you trust more to understand than one who has gone through it all before you? And **yes, even in the midst of it all, you can mourn in joy!**

The joy does not come from feeling happy. Feelings are part of your earthly soul. The joy comes from a deep knowledge down in the centre of your spirit that God loves you and will turn it all into good if you allow Him to use you and mold you into the image of His Son. God has always taken the foolish, the lowly, the people who were not exactly the most powerful or most popular and made them into a tool to save others.

God used Joseph, *a boy who did not know when to keep his mouth shut*, to save his own family. Imagine having a dream where all your brothers were bowing down to you and then having the nerve to tell them about it! It does not justify their act of throwing him into a well and then eventually selling him to a passing caravan on its way to Egypt. And yet God took Joseph and put him in **exactly** the right spot **at the right time** so that when famine came he could provide his family with food! The story is found in the Bible in Genesis 37.

God took Rebecca and our family and allowed us the privilege of being there for Tedd when his own family couldn't because they were thousands of miles away!

God took Moses from his mother before he even knew her and placed him in the family of the pharaoh to learn leadership skills to prepare him to lead the Israelites to the Promised Land.

The Bible is filled with stories of unimportant people like fishermen and tax collectors being used to change their world. And if you allow Him to, he will use you too! Now I would like to tell you the story about '*The Investor*'. Do you wonder what on earth that topic has to do with the rest of this book? *Invest* a little time reading it. You will see!

CHARLES G. PEDLEY

16 *The Investor*

Once there was a man who over his lifetime learned a strategy of investing which made him a multi-billionaire. As he was getting on in age, he wished to pass on this knowledge to his children and all those who would be patient enough to learn the technique.

He knew that if he sat them down and told them how he did it, they would forget and give up too soon or remember only part of it, so he decided to write a book called the **The Investor's Manual**.

In this book, he laid out, in specific detail, chapter after chapter the technique he had used to become so rich. It was a long book. He explained a method and then gave examples of how it had worked in his own life. Knowing that all of his children think differently, he explained the same principles in several different ways, hoping that if they did not understand and believe after reading one way, that maybe, just maybe they would finally read a method that they understood. It was not a short book. It took several years to write, but finally it was finished and was published.

That year, at Christmas he gave each of his children a copy of his book, hot off the press. They all thanked their dad very much for the gift as is the custom at Christmas. Some of them started reading it and thought it was too simple; others began and thought, "**This is too boring**! Maybe I will read it when I get older!" Some would read a chapter, try the idea they had read and when it did not work out right away, give up in disgust.

A few of them patiently read on. After all, their dad was a multi-billionaire. He must know something! Even though parts of it made no sense, these patient ones kept reading until they had finished the whole book. Some even read parts of it again and again.

A few decided to take a little of their money and try what dad had told them. They didn't became rich overnight, but gradually those who kept studying **The Investor's Manual** and investing according to the principles that their dad had laid out, came to see that it worked. They discovered the ideas that their dad had discovered over his lifetime and put them into practice. Ever so slowly they became richer and richer. Even though it had taken dad his lifetime to learn, they learned at a younger age and started to accumulate wealth sooner.

Some of the children who had not finished the book thought that dad had given the wealthy ones more money to start with and became jealous and envious. They would stay away from family gatherings because they were angry that Dad would be more generous to some than others. The family grew further and further apart.

Finally, one of the children who had become a multi-millionaire at an early age thought that he would try to bring the family back together again like it had been when they were young. **He called a meeting and told them that he would tell them exactly how he accumulated so much wealth. They all came even though it had been a long time since they had been together.**

He shared with them one of the principles that had made him wealthy. Then he gave each one of his family $10, 000 and told them to go and try it and not to give up too soon.

They all took the money. Some thought they could think of better ways to use the money and decided to spend it on a 'good time'. Some invested the money like their brother had said and waited.

Results did not always come immediately. But for those who were patient, they began to see their money grow! **Dad's ideas did work after all**! After seeing that **even one** idea made money for them, some of them searched and searched until they found their copy of **The Investor's Manual** and started to read it again.

Every time they put a principle into practice, with patience, they discovered that it accumulated more money and gradually their fortunes grew. They became wealthier and wealthier like their dad had been. They discovered that dad's ideas worked after all but not always right away or as soon as you would like. Some of them take time and patience to ride out the storm so to speak and not give up.

You will immediately recognize the name of the father when I tell you. His name is Almighty Father, Creator, Mighty God, and Everlasting Father. And you have probably guessed it by now, that **The Investor's Manual** is like the Bible.

And now you know the rest of the story! If you look back you will see various ways that we react to the Bible, God's method *of living* to us. In fact, some may have put this article down and decided to read it later just the way we often do with the Bible! And of course ***The Investor's Manual*** was a great Christmas gift! The son who put his father's method into practice was of course, Jesus, our greatest Christmas gift ever! Many billions since have followed his example, as best they could, as imperfect human beings and their lives have been changed for the better.

Do you see how we let preconceived ideas influence our thoughts and actions? Do you see that it is our attitude toward things that happen to us that determines how we think and feel and ultimately, act? ***Do you see how changing our attitude and giving a new attitude a chance can change your life?*** It has changed mine many times! Sometimes I am just downright stupid! It takes God allowing things to happen in my life again and again to finally get the message through this thick skull of mine! I will give you a recent example.

About two years ago in the spring, on the way back from Virginia; we made a wrong turn at night and found ourselves on an unfamiliar highway. The weather had turned foul; snowy, slushy driving had set in. I was driving about 45 or 50 miles per hour. It seemed like a safe speed at the time. Suddenly, as we turned a corner I could feel our minivan losing its grip on the road beneath. **Black ice!** It had looked clear! In those few seconds I don't exactly know what I did but I must have touched the brakes. That sent us spinning in a 360 degree circle ending up in the ditch on the wrong side of the road, *facing the traffic.*

I tried my door, but it was wedged in by the snow. My daughter on the opposite side of the Villager could get out. But before she did a man in a red pickup stopped on the other side of the highway and asked us if we were okay. We said yes, but we would need a tow. He just happened to have a winch on the back of his truck. After the traffic had cleared, he hooked up and with a little help from the Villager, we were out!

I don't know how the others felt but I was very thoughtful and a little shaky for the next while. Thoughts came to my mind. What if we had been too close to traffic when we started spinning? What if a transport truck (which appeared just after the gentleman stopped) had been only two minutes sooner? We could have easily had a head-on crash! Perhaps at my age of 57, someone was trying to tell me to slow down even more than I felt I could handle!

The second part of this story occurred on a Friday, early in April 2003, the year I am writing this. We were on our way to Massachusetts to visit our first daughter, Ann and her family. There had been freezing rain which turned into rain. The speed of the traffic increased as did mine.

My wife and I were deep in conversation about something. I failed to notice that the trees at the side of the road once again were covered with ice. The road appeared almost bare, but as we arrived at the top of a hill where Route 90 took a left curve, I felt that awful feeling again. The Villager was sliding.

Suddenly we were in another spin, at a higher speed than two years before. Black ice again! We did a 180 degree turn, hitting the guardrail with the back corner of the driver's side. Then, we must have swung back with the force of the hit and the front driver's corner slammed against the rail. We bounced back and came to a stop. I found my foot on the brake again. *Since then I have read that in a front-wheel drive vehicle you should actually accelerate a little when you feel that you are going to skid. A most unnatural thing to do!*

We were facing the wrong way on the paved shoulder by the guardrail. I got out to look at the damage. None of the crumpled area was touching the tire. I tried driving a little forward. It seemed okay. I watched for a break in the traffic and did a 180 degree turn over onto the shoulder of the median facing the right direction. Within a minute a yellow highway vehicle came along and phoned the state trooper for us.

When the traffic had died down, we drove slowly toward Albany. Everything worked fine. We stayed overnight and continued the next day to Massachusetts. I reported the accident to my insurance company. I knew from looking at the crumpled mess of steel and broken light parts that it would cost at least $6000 or more to repair it. Our Villager was 10 years old with over 360,000 km on it and was waiting its time to be retired anyway. If the Mercury Villager had not been in an accident, the most we could have sold it for would have been $1000 - $1500.

When we returned home, the insurance adjuster phoned after looking at the vehicle and stated that **we would get a check for $4784** to replace it. I jumped for joy and thanked God. He took a bad situation again and made it good!

But why did I tell you this? I did a lot of thinking over the few days after the accident. First, we have an accident with no injuries or damage, then we have damage to our vehicle. Was God trying to give me a message that next time one of us could be hurt? That is how I took it. I guess at the age of 59, I had to be even more careful than I used to be when I was younger.

But I am still amazed how God took that accident to give me a message and yet still bring us over $3,000 more than we expected!

Perhaps God has tried to give you messages too. Were you listening? I hope you are!

If you commit your life to Him, He takes bad things and turns them into good! He took a 'tragedy' in the life of my young daughter and brought good out of it! ***Will you allow Him to take your bad things and turn them to good? He is only a prayer away!***

Note: For extra help, photos, and useful links and references please see my site below. Also read ***Elizabeth's Story*** on the website Joyful Mourning or http://www.joyfulmourning.com **In fact, you can even hear Tedd do a drum solo!**

Appendix A:
Do You Have Anxiety?

By **Dr. Bill Gaultiere**[5]
Executive Director of New Hope

Here's a short self-test to help you see if you (or a loved one) *might* have a problem with **"ANXIETY."** This is a simple screening tool to identify key symptoms of anxiety disorders. Keep track of your "yes" answers, circling any of the seven symptoms that have one or more yes answers.

1. <u>A gitated?</u> Are you easily frustrated or irritated or upset? Do you lose your temper often?
2. <u>N ot sleeping?</u> Are you having trouble getting to sleep or staying asleep? Do you often wake up and not feel rested?
3. <u>X —fears?</u> Do you have any fears that you accommodate by avoiding situations? Are you afraid of social situations, interpersonal conflict, rejection, failure, public speaking, leaving home, airplanes, spiders, knives, etc.?
4. <u>I n your body?</u> Have you been experiencing shortness of breath, heart palpitations, tightness in your chest, discomfort in your stomach or bowels, twitching, shaking hands, sweaty palms, or tingling?

---

[5]As of September 2012 Dr. Bill has several ministries, <u>Soul Shepherding</u>, and <u>Christian Soul Care</u>. For more about him, see **http://www.christiansoulcare.com/about/bill-gaultiere/** and a co-founder of <u>New Hope Online</u> counseling site at http://www.newhopenow.org/about/index.html.

5. **E** scalating worries? Are you worried about problems you're facing? Do your thoughts race out of control?
6. **T** raumas relived? Does your mind keep re-experiencing an upsetting event(s)? Are you having nightmares?
7. **Y** es all the time? Do you feel pressured to say yes to other people, to your perfectionism, or to make troubling thoughts go away?

Scoring: Two or more yes answers suggest you may have a problem with anxiety. For diagnoses and treatment consult in person with a doctor or psychotherapist

Appendix B: Are You Depressed?

Dr. Bill Gaultiere[6]

Here's a short self-test to help you see if you (or a loved one) might be "DEPRESSED." This is a simple screening tool to identify key symptoms of clinical depression. Keep track of your "yes" answers, circling any of the nine symptoms that have one or more yes answers.

1. D ifficulty sleeping, eating, or sexually? Are you sleeping too much or not enough? Are you overeating or have you lost your appetite? Has your sex drive diminished significantly or gone into overdrive?
2. E nergy-less? Do you feel tired most of the time? Are you having trouble feeling motivated to do the things you need to do?
3. P essimism about your future? Do you feel negative about what's ahead for you? Do you feel hopeless?
4. R egrets about your past? Do you feel bad when you think about things you've done in the past? Are you struggling with guilt?
5. E njoyment gone? Have you lost a sense of pleasure in your relationships, activities, and hobbies? Does life feel more like a chore than a joy?

---

[6] New Hope Counseling Center - Crystal Cathedral Ministries

6. S ad? Are you experiencing unexpected tearfulness? Do you feel unhappy much of the time?

7. S elf-critical? Are you quick to criticize your mistakes? Are you often harsh with yourself?
8. E mpty? Do you feel a sense of emptiness? Does your life feel mundane or lacking in meaning?
9. D ecisions difficult? Are you having trouble deciding what you need to do in situations? Are you having problems concentrating?

Scoring: Three or more "YES" answers suggest that you may have a problem with depression. For diagnoses or treatment, consult in person with a doctor or psychotherapist.

Appendix C: Life Stress Test

Used by permission of Dr. Tim Lowenstein[7]

In the past 12 months, which of the following major life events have taken place in your life?
1. Make a check mark next to each event that you have experienced this year.
2. When you're done, add up the points for each event.
3. Check your score at the bottom.

_____ Death of Spouse 100
_____ Divorce 73
_____ Marital Separation 65
_____ Jail Term 63
_____ Death of close family member 63
_____ Personal injury or illness 53
_____ Marriage 50
_____ Fired from work 47
_____ Marital reconciliation 45
_____ Retirement 45
_____ Change in family member's health 44
_____ Pregnancy 40
_____ Sex difficulties 39
_____ Addition to family 39
_____ Business readjustment 39
_____ Change in financial status 38
_____ Death of close friend 37
_____ Change to a different line of work 36
_____ Change in number of marital arguments 35

---

[7] Conscious Living Foundation is found at http://www.cliving.org/ . Conscious Living Foundation, P.O. Box 9, Drain, OR 97435

_____ Mortgage or loan over $10,000 31
_____ Foreclosure of mortgage or loan 30
_____ Change in work responsibilities 29
_____ Trouble with in-laws 29
_____ Outstanding personal achievement 28
_____ Spouse begins or stops work 26
_____ Starting or finishing school 26
_____ Change in living conditions 25
_____ Revision of personal habits 24
_____ Trouble with boss 23
_____ Change in work hours, conditions 20
_____ Change in residence 20
_____ Change in schools 20
_____ Change in recreational habits 19
_____ Change in church activities 19
_____ Change in social activities 18
_____ Mortgage or loan under $10,000 17
_____ Change in sleeping habits 16
_____ Change in number of family gatherings 15
_____ Change in eating habits 15
_____ Vacation 13
_____ Christmas season 12
_____ Minor violations of the law 11
_____ Your Total Score

LIFE STRESS SCORES

0-149 Low susceptibility to stress-related illness
150-299 Medium susceptibility to stress-related illness.
Learn and practice relaxation and stress management skills and a healthy well life style.
300 and over High susceptibility to stress-related illness
Daily practice of relaxation skills is very important for your wellness. Take care of it now before a serious illness erupts or an affliction becomes worse.

This scale shows the kind of life pressure that you are facing. Depending on your coping skills or the lack there of, this scale can predict the likelihood of you falling victim to a stress related illness. The illness could be mild (like frequent tension headaches, acid indigestion, loss of sleep) or very serious illness (like ulcers, cancer, migraines and the like.)

CHARLES G. PEDLEY

Appendix D: What is Your Image of God?

By Dr. Bill Gaultiere,
Executive Director of New Hope

Here's a self-test I developed called the *"God Image Questionnaire" (GIQ).* The GIQ is meant to help you better understand how you see God on an emotional level. Each question asks about your *feelings* in your relationship with God. Please answer according to your feelings or *experiences* and not your opinions or beliefs about God. Read each question and then circle "T" for true and "F" for false.

1. At times I feel that God doesn't give His full attention to the details of my life. T F
2. When I need God it sometimes feels like He does not help me very much. T F
3. I feel like God sometimes withholds good things from me. T F
4. I feel disregarded by God at times. T F
5. I feel that God is distant from me. T F
6. At times I feel pressured to do something for God that I don't want to do. T F
7. I feel I have to do something to obtain God's favor. T F
8. To please God I feel I must measure up to His expectations. T F
9. When I confess my sin I don't always feel forgiven by God. T F
10. At times it feels unfair the way God treats me. T F

11. If I'm in a threatening situation I tend to feel unprotected by God. T F
12. I feel that my abilities are unimportant to God. T F
13. I feel unsure about whether or not God has a purpose for my future. T F
14. When I really need God I tend to feel left on my own. T F
15. I feel that I may be a bother to God if I talk to Him about a decision I need to make. T F
16. I feel that I don't get enough help with my problems from God. T F
17. At times I feel deprived of good things by God. T F
18. I feel insignificant to God. T
19. I feel removed from God. T
20. Sometimes I feel controlled by God. T F
21. If I want God to do something for me then it feels like it helps my cause to do something for Him. T F
22. I feel disapproved of by God. T F
23. After I tell God I am sorry I still feel He may be upset with me. T F
24. I feel harshly judged by God sometimes. T F
25. If someone tries to take advantage of me I tend to feel undefended by God. T F
26. I feel that my abilities are doubted by God. T F
27. I feel unsure of whether or not God has special plans for my future. T F
28. In difficult times it feels like God isn't at my side. T F

Scoring: To score and understand your GIQ use the table below. It has 14 rows, one for each of the 14 aspects of God's perfect love from 1 Corinthians 13:4-7. (The first word or term for each aspect of love is from the NIV translation and the other words are my definitions.) There are two questions ("Quest") for each aspect.

"False" answers to any question on the GIQ indicate a generally and usually positive experience of God's love (or image of God) in that particular aspect.

Follow these four steps:

1. Circle each of the 28 questions that you answered with "false."

2. Count one point for each "false" answer.

3. Add up the total for each row (aspect of God's love). Scores should range from 0 to 2. Scores of 2 indicate your God Image strengths, areas where you have a positive experience of that aspect of God's love. Scores of 0 indicate your God Image weaknesses, areas where you're struggling to feel God's love and need help.

4. Add up your total GIQ score for all 14 rows combined. Scores should range from 0 to 28. Higher scores mean a closer and more loving relationship with God, an image of God that is more positive and true to the God of the Bible

Question	**Aspect of God's Love**	Score
1,15	Patient: attentive, interested	
2,16	Kind: helpful	
3,17	Not envious: generous, gives good gifts	
4,18	Not boastful: esteems and shows regard	
5,19	Not proud: close, available	
6,20	Not rude: gives freedom, gentle	
7,21	Not self-seeking: unconditional favor and care	
8,22	Not easily angered: considerate of weaknesses	
9,23	No record of wrongs: forgiving, merciful	
10,24	Rejoices in truth, not evil: fair, does what's right	
11,25	Protects: keeps safe, defends	
12,26	Trusts: respects, believes in abilities	
13,27	Hopeful: has good plan and purpose	
14,28	Perseveres: reliable, faithful	
	GIQ Total	

Appendix E: Do You Esteem Yourself?

Dr. Bill Gaultiere
Executive Director of New Hope

Here's a short self-test to help you see how well esteem yourself. Each question asks how you respond to a particular situation. Keep track of your "yes" answers.

1. Can you maintain good feelings about yourself even if someone criticizes you?
2. When you fail or do something wrong can you say you're sorry and accept forgiveness or do you persist in feeling bad about yourself?
3. Can you offer a dissenting opinion to people you respect?
4. If you talked to one of your children or to your best friend the way you talk to yourself would they feel esteemed?
5. Do you say thank you when you're complemented?
6. Do you avoid comparing yourself to others, thinking that you're better than or less than they are?
7. When you've been hurt do you receive comfort from yourself and others instead of hiding your pain?
8. If your spouse, roommate, or someone you're close to is in a bad mood do you maintain your

own feelings of well-being anyway (without matching their mood)?
9. Do you know what your gifts and talents are and are you confident using them?
10. Can you say "good enough" about a project you're working on instead of being perfectionistic?
11. Do you appreciate your strengths and work to improve your weaknesses instead of overlooking your strengths and feeling bad about your weaknesses?

Scoring: The more yes answers you have, the stronger your self-esteem. Eight or more yes answers suggest that your self-esteem is in good shape. Each no answer indicates an area that you need to work on in order to strengthen your self-esteem.

Appendix F: Do You Overreact Emotionally?

-Dr. Bill Gaultiere

Here's a short self-test to help you identify if you (or a loved one) may have a problem with emotional reactivity.

1. Are you quick to lose your temper?

2. When you lose your temper do you yell, say demeaning things, or become physically violent?

3. Do you make critical or sarcastic comments that are hurtful to others?

4. Do you express 100 volts of emotion (anger, fear, tearfulness, or shame) when 10 are appropriate?

5. Do others describe you as moody? Does your mood swing up and down?

6. Do you have anxiety attacks?

7. Are you overcome with sudden floods of tears?

8. Do you say or do things that you're embarrassed about later?

9. Do you make big decisions impulsively, without much thought?

10. Do other people walk on egg shells around you because they're afraid to upset you?

Yes answers to three or more questions suggest that you're reacting negatively to emotional situations. Overreacting is probably causing you significant problems in your relationships, decision-making, or work. Read my article, "Think with Your Heart, Feel with Your Head" and consider talking with a counsellor.

Dr. Bill Gaultiere is the Director of New Hope Crisis Counselling at the Crystal Cathedral and a Psychologist with ChristianSoulCare.com.

Appendix G
What is Your Emotional IQ?

Dr. Bill Gaultiere

Each question asks how you act or feel in certain situations. For each one answer how often it is true of your actual (not desired) behavior or attitude.

1. When I feel bad I don't know exactly what or who is bothering me.

    Always (3) Usually (5) Sometimes (7) Rarely (9) Never (11)

2. When faced with a disappointment or a loss I try not to feel sad.

    Always (3) Usually (5) Sometimes (7) Rarely (9) Never (11)

3. I put high priority on how I feel when I make an important decision.

    Always (3) Usually (5) Sometimes (7) Rarely (9) Never (11)

4. There are a number of things that I don't like about myself.

    Always (3) Usually (5) Sometimes (7) Rarely (9) Never (11)

5. When I am upset it takes a long time for me to feel better.

    Always (3) Usually (5) Sometimes (7) Rarely (9) Never (11)

6. When someone criticizes me unfairly I feel bad about myself.

    Always (3) Usually (5) Sometimes (7) Rarely (9) Never (11)

7. I say things to others that I regret later.

    Always (3) Usually (5) Sometimes (7) Rarely (9) Never (11)

8. I lose my temper or fume in silence when I get angry.

    Always (3) Usually (5) Sometimes (7) Rarely (9) Never (11)

9. My emotions are up and down.

    Always (3) Usually (5) Sometimes (7) Rarely (9) Never (11)

10. When someone shares a problem with me I think more about how he/she could solve it than about how difficult it feels for him/her.

    Always (3) Usually (5) Sometimes (7) Rarely (9) Never (11)

11. I have trouble handling conflicts with other people.

    Always (3) Usually (5) Sometimes (7) Rarely (9) Never (11)

12. I am unable to sense other people's unspoken feelings on important issues.

    Always (3) Usually (5) Sometimes (7) Rarely (9) Never (11)

13. It's hard for me to wait to get what I want even if I should.

    Always (3) Usually (5) Sometimes (7) Rarely (9) Never (11)

14. When working on a challenge I struggle to feel hopeful, energetic, and confident.

    Always (3) Usually (5) Sometimes (7) Rarely (9) Never (11)

15. If I have to do something I don't want to do I put it off till later.

    Always (3) Usually (5) Sometimes (7) Rarely (9) Never (11)

Scores range from 45 to 165 with 105 being average. 120 and above is exceptional.

Dr. Bill Gaultiere was the Director of New Hope Crisis Counselling at the Crystal Cathedral.

He is a Psychologist at **ChristianSoulCare.com** for individuals and **SoulShepherding.org** for those in

Ministry

> **Griefshare** - **http://www.griefshare.org/** - I mention this because recently my friend who was helped when we went up north lost his wife. He heard about **Griefshare** through his church and found it a VERY helpful program to help those who are mourning and those who should be mourning but have kept it all inside where it can only do harm when it is finally released in an ugly form. I have also heard good things about it from others.

CHARLES G. PEDLEY

Appendix H: Links to Help You Cope

I must give the website below much credit for many of the links and articles in the appendix.

http://www.newhopenow.com/ - A ministry of the Crystal Cathedral. You can get live help online if you wish. Many articles plus Robert Schuler's wonderfully positive upbuilding messages can encourage you.

www.joyfulmourning.com will take you to my website to encourage those who are grieving.

Stress Management

International Stress Management Association: Network for various professional groups and helpful library of articles for the public, www.stress-management-isma.org.

National Center for Post-Traumatic Stress Disorder: Help for veterans, trauma survivors, and others, **1-802-296-5132**, www.ncptsd.org/Index.html.

Crisis Intervention

American Association of Suicidology: Help for survivors of suicide, those in crisis, and crisis counselors, **1-202-237-2280,** www.suicidology.org/things.htm.

Hankinson Interventions: Christian service coordinates interventions for addicts and those acting irresponsibly, **1-800-894-9307.**

National Suicide Prevention Hotline: 24-hour suicide prevention, **1-800-SUICIDE,** (784-2433).

New Hope Crisis Counselling: Suicide prevention, general support, self-help articles, and referrals offered by Christian volunteers, **1-714-NEW-HOPE** (639-4673), www.newhopenow.org.

New Hope Teenline: Christian teenagers offer suicide prevention, support, and referrals for other teenagers, 24-hour, **(714)639-8336**, www.teenline.org.

Prison Fellowship Ministry: Christian ministry to prisoners, crime victims, and their families, **1-877-478-0100,** www.pfm.org.

Depression

Bipolar Disorders Information Center: Information and support groups for those with manic-depression, www.mhsource.com/bipolar.

Depression: Diagnostic and treatment information for the depressed and their families, NIMH, www.nimh.nih.gov/publicat/depressionmenu.cfm.

Depression and Bipolar Support Alliance: Information and support groups, 1-800-826-3632, www.dbsalliance.org.

Emotions Anonymous: Information and support groups, **1-651-647-9712,** www.emotionsanonymous.org.

National Foundation for Depressive Illness: Information on the steps to getting better, **1-800-239-1265,** www.depression.org.

Appendix I
Mental Health & Counselling

Griefshare - http://www.griefshare.org/ - I mention this because recently my friend who was helped when we went up north lost his wife. He heard about Griefshare through his church and found it a VERY helpful program to help those who are mourning and those who should be mourning but have kept it all inside where it can only do harm when it is finally released in an ugly form. I have also heard good things about it from others.

American Association of Christian Counselors: Find a local AACC registered counsellor or pastor, **1-800-526-8673,** www.aacc.net.

Autism Society of America: Information for the autistic and their families, 1-800-3AUTISM (328-8476), www.autism-society.org.

Emotions Anonymous: Information and support groups, **1-651-647-9712,** www.emotionsanonymous.org.

False Memory Syndrome Foundation: Information on false memories and support for those affected by it, **1-214-940-1040,** www.fmsfonline.org.

Focus on the Family: Find a local Christian therapist, **1-800-A-FAMILY**

Healthy Place: Communities and information for many psychological and relational interests and concerns, www.healthyplace.com.

International Society for the Study of Dissociation: Information for professionals and the public on dissociative states (including multiple personality disorder), www.issd.org.

Internet Mental Health: Peer counseling, diagnostic descriptions for all mental disorders, helpful information, www.mentalhealth.com.

Mental Wellness: Information, testimonies, and resources, www.mentalwellness.com.

Medications: Psychotropic drug information and education from NIMH, www.nimh.nih.gov/publicat/medicate.cfm.

Multiplicity, Abuse, & Healing Network: Resources on Multiple Personality Disorder, dissociation, various forms of abuse including ritual abuse, self-harm, and emotional healing, www.m-a-h.net.

National Alliance for the Mentally Ill: Meetings, information, and resources to support the family of the mentally ill, **1-800-950-6264,** www.nami.org.

National Attention Deficit Disorder Association: Information and support groups, **1-847-432-ADDA** (2332), www.add.org.

National Institute of Mental Health (NIMH): Information on specific mental disorders and treatments, www.nimh.nih.gov/publicat/index.cfm.

National Mental Health Association: Referrals and information, **1-800-969-6642,** www.nmha.org.

New Life Treatment Centers: Psychiatric Hospitals, outpatient referrals, self-help resources, **1-800- NEW-LIFE** (639-5433), www.newlife.com.

Overcomers Outreach: Christian support groups, **1-800-310-3001,** www.overcomersoutreach.org.

Personality Types: Understanding and getting along with different personality types, descriptions of Myers-Briggs types, and online questionnaire by Keirsey to determine type, www.keirsey.com.

Recovery Options Network: Chemical dependency & psychiatric referrals of all types (including low fee referrals), sponsored by Christian-based Pacific Hills Treatment Centers, **1-800-NO-ABUSE** (1-800-662-2873), www.pachills.com.

Schizophrenia: An abundance of helpful information for patients and families, www.schizophrenia.com.

Schizophrenic's Anonymous: Support groups and information, **1-800-482-9534,** www.sanonymous.org.

Self-Injury: Information and resources for those who cause physical injury to themselves, http://crystal.palace.net/~llama/psych/injury.html

---

Please refer to my book website at
www.joyfulmourning.com
for updated help links and additions.

> Be sure to read **Elizabeth's story**. Elizabeth came into the Shiloh youth group just as Tedd and Rebecca started their ministry.
> The story is on the website above.
>
> **Elizabeth** actually has now become an author as well! You will see the reference to her book on the web page.

> **My prayer for you is that YOU may experience the process of *Joyful Mourning* as we have! May God bless you!**

Reward Offered!

Please feel free to write to me at cp@cpedley.com for any of the following reasons:
- you find a bad link
- you have any questions or comments
- you have an extra link you have found that would be helpful to others.
- you have any questions about the book
- you comment on the book on Amazon

The Reward!

A **FREE EBOOK** copy of *Joyful Mourning – A True Love Story.*

Maybe there is someone you know who needs help.

JOYFUL MOURNING

My main reference website is at **www.cpedley.com**. You will also find there links to many of my other blogs usually designed to help people in various ways.

- **Schoolgenius.com** to give hope to students
- **Doc-computer.com** to help you with computers
- **Financial Peace** to help with finances
- **Press4Truth.com** to highlight current events
- **Saving-a-Dollar.com** to help with finances
- **Press4fun.com** to give you a good clean laugh
- **Allipedia** - divergent compendium of knowledge
- **Churchmall.ca**
- **Churchmart.ca**
- **ChurchFurnitureCanada.ca**
- and more ... :)

www.ingramcontent.com/pod-product-compliance
Lightning Source LLC
Chambersburg PA
CBHW071501040426
42444CB00008B/1437

Part 4: Resilience

Chapter 7: The "D" Word

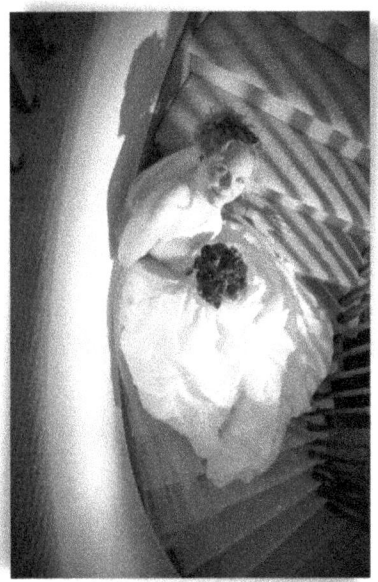

How many of us right now are in marriages that are very misaligned? How many of us sit knowing that the person on this life path with us now, is no longer the person we want to be with and yet we don't really see a clear path forward? And how many of us are sticking around simply for our children...

My divorce caused challenges as I grew through the change of a different chapter forward. But now the peace we both feel and the love beaming from our children tell me it was, in the end, the right way forward. I wouldn't change what is, and our children wouldn't change what is; we can all talk about the past without crying and actually say that we're better off the way it is now.

I know it's hard financially to do these things, especially now. And yet, if we choose to stay in a misaligned relationship, the impact it has on all of us long-term will be a wake-up call that comes too late. I don't want to write this and yet I will because I feel it's truly impactful and will guide you forward differently as a result of me saying it on paper. I believe that the reason I got sick is because I was so misaligned in my marriage (and other areas), and I was resisting what the universe needed me to do.

What if staying in your marriage is making you sick? What if staying in your marriage is making your children more and more angry and resentful too?

Until death do us part...I actually believed it. For better or worse, my ex-husband and I worked, until we didn't. We were on the path to success but it was really a never-ending misalignment growing bigger and bigger. I am so sad to have walked away from my marriage. I worked my a** off to work together, however, it wasn't enough.

As I came out of my wake-up call, after being diagnosed, I was different and there was no going back to the "OLD Nancy" which I know is what ultimately ended our marriage. I chose that day to unravel it all and learn how to change my brain, how to become a calm and peaceful human being, and that person wasn't the one who stood at the altar taking marriage vows. Old Nancy wanted the big job and the big career path..."NEW Nancy" required something different, something she didn't even know yet.

In order to find the "NEW Nancy". I needed to unravel my whole life up until then and rebuild from the ground up. I sought the help of a life coach and quickly realized that my marriage was a huge barrier. I saw huge gaps in what we wanted for our lives. I was focused on creating a life free of sickness, but from the inside out rather than treating it from the outside in with medication. The moment I decided I couldn't be a superwoman anymore, my marriage ended.

But it wasn't just one moment, it was all the little moments that led to our demise. As we faced harder and harder things, it was clear we were not moving forward together. I watched myself fall into a deep hole and didn't know how to get out and watched him do the same. Resentment set in. The difference between the plan we had versus the reality was too great. And I can't blame either of us for that. I chose healing and became a different version while I was healing. Then we just existed, side by side.

We are not taught to deal with the hard stuff. When hard things happen, communication is ultimately tested. Even with both my ex-husband and I being good communicators, somewhere along the way we started to veer apart and the gap got so big that we couldn't come back.

"F" Words

So many of us have faked life for so long that we don't even know who we are anymore...we fake it in the effort to gain CONTROL but lack of control and uncertainty creates FEAR. I call this "F." I GET IT...I once lived there too. FAKE might seem great on the surface, but it's exhausting and it will catch up with you. Pretending takes away your energy. The more you fake it, the more you feel you have to fake it, the more you surround yourself with fake. Then, you FEAR you're not faking it as well as everyone else, so you FAKE some more.

And now, as these last 2 years have flown by, I am so excited to see another word finally emerging...one that I love talking about.

The L mentality...

- Love
- Light

- Let go...

And if "F" comes into the picture...it's because F*CK is said with a SMILE...because it feels EMPOWERING. And of course, FAITH is at the forefront...with FORGIVENESS as the ultimate superpower. The only difference between the people using the "F" mentality vs. "L" mentality is CHOICE. The "L" people have lived in the "F" place...however they used their learnings to flow into the "L" place.

Now, they don't always live in the "L" place and do things perfectly from a place of "L", however, they grow and learn from their mistakes...and use compassion to act from LOVE instead of ANGER.

If we get stuck in "F," the opportunity lies in becoming aware of the ROLE you play by living your life in "F," and the opportunity you have right now to see and do it differently.

What's in Your Backpack?

The analogy of the backpack resonates with me and has guided my journey to unravelling it all...maybe it will empower you.

We all carry an imaginary backpack full of "stuff." One of my most amazing coaches taught me this: the stuff we carry around is our stories and our experiences of life. This heaviness sits on our shoulders, it's why so many of us have back and shoulder pain. We, as humans right now, are carrying the weight of our worlds on our shoulders and it's time we become aware of what we are choosing to carry.

My ex and I got to the point where, unfortunately, there was so much baggage; we came home to the safe space that was our family and it all leaked out. I see so many of us doing this: faking our happiness out in the world and then going home to our safe place, but now it's a place of anger, sadness, and resentment because that's the only place we can let it out. It's only now when I look back on my marriage that I see the pivotal moments that changed us. At the time, I couldn't see it because of our ability to cope, which ironically is one of our greatest assets as human beings. What if we had taken the time to unravel our emotional baggage, rather than just cope, in those pivotal moments? I wish that we had taken the time to do things differently and yet, 3 years later on the other side, I see the reasons why we weren't able to do it differently. And I think we are both aligning better with our true selves and my children are much better off now than they were with us married and unhappy.

If we choose to always carry around our backpacks and never pop them open, then we live most of our lives in the "F" zone with anger, blame, judgement, etc. What matters most about your story, about your experiences, is what you learn and what you choose to do with them. You don't have to carry the weight of your experiences—you can carry just the lessons you've learned which are much LIGHTER.

Forgiveness

I walked out the month before COVID-19, February 2020, after literally asking the universe for a break. What I learned is this: work on yourself and then if he follows great, if not, you'll know. I'm sad when people walk away instead of working on themselves. Anger eats away at you so you need to FORGIVE in order to move on.

During COVID-19 I went inward, I could sit in anger or I could sit in choice. I had to sit in my sh*t and figure it out. It was the worst 3 years of my life but also the best 3 years of my life.

Society teaches us that if we have everything in order then we have control and everything will be okay. Our experiences, the bad ones maybe most of all, force you to go from heart to head, or logic. We focus on our brains as the CONTROL centres rather than listening to our hearts. Our generation is letting go of the illusion of control, but we're not sure what that looks like exactly. These moments of trauma are tests to surrender control. LET IT GO.

Forgiveness is the key. Forgive your ex. Forgive your kids. Forgive your parents. Most importantly, forgive YOURSELF.

Freedom comes when we learn to acknowledge ourselves first. When, instead of looking at a situation from the perspective of what others did, you take a look inward to discover what triggered it all in the first place.

- Love flows when we allow what is to be.
- Love is the path to forgiveness.
- Love flows when we accept what has happened and forgive ourselves for the role we played.
- Love flows when we have peace in our HEARTS for everything that has happened, regardless of how sh*tty it is.

For me, love and forgiveness go hand in hand, as you truly cannot love deeper until you take the time to acknowledge what is coming up and choose to see/feel it differently. In the choice to do differently, we find space in the present moment, which is where we can flow differently.

- Forgiveness is the one emotion that truly requires TIME AND patience and it is necessary in order to heal.
- It's a process.
- It's daily awareness and a commitment to lean in rather than run from.
- It's taking time to go inward, seeing the spaces where you have those icky feelings, and making a choice to do something different with them.

For me, it started with writing my true authentic feelings down…I wrote letters. I expressed my words out loud…and then I acknowledged my own responsibility for those moments…

Then, it was the HARD part–to feel what I was meant to feel all that time ago. To stop blaming others and instead take a look in the mirror to see what role I played. To go back to the time in my life where I felt it and feel it from a place of now - with compassion.

At the time, I didn't know how to do it differently…now I do.

Many call this inner child work…for me, I call it making peace with self. Making peace with self is going inward vs. outward. Making peace is BEING In the NOW…and almost working backwards. I now have tools for my forgiveness process. As you start allowing those moments of NOW you rise. They may help you…or you may discover your own process is different.

Ho'oponopono (Chapter 11), a prayer of forgiveness, has been my key to letting go and releasing. Words have immense power for our mind, our body, and our soul. Forgiveness of self is the antidote to it all…I try to be aware every day of how I TALK to other people and, more importantly, how I talk to myself and forgive myself.

We have a choice only in the now. If we dwell on anything else, we are wasting valuable time so feel, release, let go, forgive, and surrender…

LOVE

As I've become more of an "L" person, my life has completely changed. Things come and go, flowing into my life and away. I don't hold onto things anymore and that's something I never imagined I could FEEL. I don't always live in "L"s, however, every moment I make a conscious effort to be aware when I flow in "F"s and shift my focus.

How do you start flowing in "L," you ask?

It's very simple. Use everything around you as a MIRROR. Stop looking at life as good or bad and start accepting it for what is. Everything and everyone is a mirror of you—when we become aware of who we are through others and grow from it, magic happens. Miracles happen. Unconditional love happens. For yourself and then everything around you, including your kids.

There is no right or wrong on whether you are an "L" or "F" person. But remember that whatever you put out into the world is what you will receive. If you want to receive love, then you must show love.

HEART: Unpack Your Backpack

What are you carrying in your backpack right now? What experiences in your life do you still have to let go? What conversations do you find yourself having over and over again? What do you dream about frequently? Unpack your backpack by listing some of these core experiences, what you learned from those experiences and how they might be holding you back.

_____
_____
_____
_____
_____
_____
_____
_____
_____
_____

Chapter 8: Another "F" Word

The word F*CK...this word is my ultimate superpower. When added to any word, it can shift an entire moment. Out of chaos and into courage. Out of anger and into laughter...

It can take a newfound friendship from uncomfortable to "I f*cking love you" within minutes, if said with a smile. It can take a word and make it magical... "Abso-f*cking-lutely" is my fav. It can take a moment of "I can't" to "F*CK it, let's do it anyway." For me, it's become my courage word.

When I'm getting ready to do something big...I often call on its power to ignite, in my body, what it needs to show up. How? By standing tall and saying it out loud. Let's do this...Remember who you are...

I am NANCY F*CKing SEIBEL
From there, I can do F*CKING ANYTHING...

To me, it's not just a word.

It has become a powerful concept that I've learned to use to guide my soul forward in all aspects of my life. After coming back from the hospital and being sh*t-scared of the diagnosis I'd been given, I knew I had no choice but to move forward and find a way to "be afraid and do it anyway"...

I knew I had to call on the warrior within and yet, I couldn't feel her anymore. I had lost myself so much in all the wrong things that I was about to give up on it all. The challenge was, I couldn't give up and you can't either...

> Regardless of how much guilt we carry—how messed up we feel or how "off kilter" our lives are—we must show up for our kids. There were SO many days I could barely stand tall this year, let alone these last 5 years, and yet my kids are the reason I stand taller, stronger, and more at peace than ever...you have this same opportunity.
>
>

If You're Not Growing, You're Shrinking

I am a grower. I am a human with a belief that everyday we must show up better than yesterday and this is NOT for ourselves anymore, but for our children. My kids and I are at the stage (12 and 14) where they call me out. I've spent years guiding them to show up as their authentic selves with kindness and truth—so I give them permission to call me out when they feel I am not aligned with the same.

I often tell my kids that just because adults wear adult suits, doesn't always mean we do it well. We too aren't perfect and we too make mistakes. Those mistakes, when we are adults, are meant to guide us to grow, to guide us to take responsibility for our own actions and more importantly, to learn from them so that we do it differently next time. Unfortunately, right now, this is NOT our number one approach in this world, and it's why I'm speaking out loud...

We cannot tell our kids to do things that we, as adults, don't do ourselves. We are their teachers, their guides, their mirrors, and if we are off kilter, or unkind to others, or judgmental of our own selves (or others), then it's pretty likely that they are going to do the same...

From the Mouths of Babes...

In my moments of hard, my daughter has come to me with a few call outs that, in the past, would have taken me out. Now, after years of practice, these moments make me realize how lucky we are as parents to have this powerful mirror that is at play.

Two times that her call outs "dug deep"...

1. "Mommy, you tell us to look you in the eyes when speaking and you've stopped. You are so

distracted by your phone and not present with us; it doesn't feel very nice"...UGH...

2. The ultimate gut-wrenching moment that really aligned me with the mirror was the day she got in the car after 2 days of anger and frustration towards each other. When I attempted to cut her off with my words, she paused and said the following: "You often say you mirror me MOM, however, I've been at school feeling all your anger and sadness today (the connection amongst kids and parents is huge) and I'm calling you out because its not me you are mirroring, it's yourself"...

Wholly F*****CK...this power of energy that flows between our kids and ourselves is magical. Kids are superpower feelers and this knowledge isn't meant to make you feel more guilty, but to empower you with the knowledge that it may be time to do something different...

So back to my favourite word. I love F*CK so much that I've built a concept around it and this concept has gotten me through the times when I can barely carry myself. When I am not mirroring my best self to the world, I no longer look outward for guidance. I go within and use this powerful concept of "F*CK IT" to find a way to do it differently.

So here it is...if you don't like swearing, FACK it works too!

F*CK IT...

F	Yell **F*********CK** really loud (or internally if you can't yell)...PAUSE, take a breath, giggle within...and **FORGIVE** yourself (you are only HUMAN).
*****	**UNDERSTAND** that you are HUMAN and that it's not what you do in the moment that matters most, it's what you do AFTER...so find a way forward differently and DO IT RIGHT NOW. If you need a friend to talk it out with, do it. Perspective is key here.
C	Learn to have **COMPASSION and CARE** for yourself in the moment. What would you say to a friend in this moment, are you saying the same to yourself???
K	We cannot "fake out" **KARMA**. We get what we give as HUMANS. If you are not showing up as your best self and not doing things wholeheartedly from a place of love and authenticity, the karma you get sucks...until you CHOOSE to do it

	differently. Accept your KARMA and try again. Learn from your KARMA, that's why it's here.
I	**"I"** - I choose in the now, I choose differently, I choose myself, I choose to…
T	**TRUST** that I am right where I'm supposed to be, that everything that happens is happening for me to grow and change.

This concept, this approach to life, has allowed me so many moments of courage to do it differently and as a result, it's completely shifted my KARMA and my life.

I offer you this same opportunity. The reality is, we are all feeling "off" right now, so the only way forward isn't to keep dwelling on what we aren't doing, but to find small ways to do it differently. What if, F*CK IT is your way forward…the time is now to try it out…

If all else fails and you get nothing out of this method, know that inserting "F*CK" between your first and last name can give you such an empowering feeling that it may be all you need to move forward.

We are all HUMAN...we all have such choices in this world and all I know is that I want my kids to do it differently than I did...which means I must reflect the ultimate in truth, acceptance, and forgiveness in my mirror...maybe it's time you did too...

F*CK it...you are so f*cking worthy of trying it out...your time is NOW.

I have a concept for kids too...it's called CHUCK IT!

Choose
How to
Understand with
Compassion and
Kindness -

I
Trust.

HEART: Cuts Like a Knife

This is an opportunity to see triggers differently…we know that words can cut like a knife. When a trigger arises, what if you paused rather than spoke, and asked for time to think about your WORDs…

What if you went home and let yourself unravel to see it differently? What words/actions have recently triggered you? Write them down.

Now, write down how you felt as a result of the trigger. Then explore why you were triggered and if you can't quite see it, sit on it and allow TIME to guide you to the answer. Once acknowledged, GO INWARD to heal that part of you that was TRIGGERed. What did you need differently at the time of the original trigger? Can you now see it differently from a place of LOVE? Can you forgive yourself for feeling that way and comfort yourself knowing you are in a different space and time? Once you HEAL through the trigger, you will NOW treat and address the situation differently, and that person will feel the difference and likely do the same. If you start to do this over and over, you will WIPE out your triggers with compassion and LOVE will flow where the trigger was once held.

HEART: Word to the Words

What's your superpower word? What words are satisfying for you to say? What words make you feel like you can do anything? Make a list here and write down a few versions of your first name and last name with your superpower words in between. Try mine out too!

_____

_____

_____

_____

_____

_____

_____

_____

_____

_____

_____

Part 5: Trust

Chapter 9: The 3Ms

When I came back from the hospital, I was scared as h*ll.

I knew I wouldn't make it in this world if I didn't get my sh*t together...the challenge? I wasn't prescribed more meds! I was prescribed a prescription that involved ME and my CHOICE as to what to do next...

Regardless of my HUGE resistance to mindfulness, I was also being asked to embrace it with open arms and find time to quiet my overthinking, insanely wonderful brain...

And, regardless of the pain I felt, I was asked to move every single day for 60 minutes and that movement was to be based on how I felt that day.

Most times, after my exercise, I had no energy to do anything else and spent the rest of the time reading, journalling, or watching TV and yet, with time, it got easier.

Two things I was asked to conquer daily—mindfulness and movement—and over time, the concept of 3M emerged.

Mindfulness

I came home with one intention—to rediscover how to take care of me.

I write this word and my entire body still goes, "I can't believe you conquered this one, Nancy!" For so many of us don't know how to sit and just BE. I was that person. I couldn't sit still, let alone be quiet enough NOT to think…and yet I was being challenged to do so…to get myself out of these patterns I had created. To learn how to do me differently.

What if you knew that the key to letting go and surrendering is listening/paying attention, and you can only do that when you get quiet enough to hear yourself. When you find the time to let what is just be and sit in it all—long enough to allow what comes to the surface. Usually, it is what we need to hear and it's magical to feel how it all happens. As I welcomed more mindfulness into my life, I realized how important it was to keep practicing and all of the sudden I was more mindful. I started meditating with a friend (for competition lol) and started experiencing moments of magic (seeing colours in my meditations, moments where my body shook to release, and moments where voices spoke to me. So many of us get uncomfortable with sitting and yet as I sat longer and longer, I started to see the reason why all of us should. The more I did it, the more my brain craved it and over time, in this last year, it's the ONE tool I can say that I use daily that has shifted it all...that has allowed me to be more in tune with the voice within that keeps speaking.

Mindfulness is HARD, especially if you are a triple A personality that can't stop and yet - if that is the case - then you REALLY need it, more than you know. For me, my mindfulness moments started with becoming more present at yoga and sitting for 5 minutes, regardless of my resistance. I found the mornings were best because my mind wouldn't resist as much. I would find something to listen to online (soothing music, nature sounds, meditations, etc.) and force myself to just sit presently. I stopped judging myself and just let myself be. Over time, I noticed these little shifts in self and more importantly - these little moments where I was choosing differently because of the calm within.

My mom says looking back that she is amazed at what I've done to rewire it all. All I knew at the time was that I no longer had a choice.

If you wish to choose mindfulness, go online today and find a 5-minute BODY SCAN meditation and force yourself to sit and BE...

If meditation isn't your thing, BREATHWORK is another way to achieve mindfulness. Breathwork is the new superpower that focuses on mind, body, and spirit which is why it has become something I often interchange with daily meditation. Research shows that it can be as effective, or more, than talk therapy.[10] Just two minutes of breathwork daily can reset your nervous system and allow you to be calm in the chaos of the day. There are many types of breathwork. I am obsessed with 9D Breathwork right now and have spent many hours doing the Wim Hoff method as well. The key is consistency and trusting that you may NOT know why you are doing it, however, when a moment of trigger hits and you respond differently, you'll start to understand. When mindfulness becomes a daily practice, you may not see the changes, but you'll FEEL them in your mood, your responses, and your actions.

---

[10] Health By Candice. (2018). Therapy vs Breathwork: A New Paradigm For Healing. Health By Candice. Retrieved from https://healthbycandice.com/blog//therapy-vs-breathwork

Movement

Whether you walk into yoga, a gym, or a CrossFit box, when you find a group that matches your vibe, you want more of it...and that's what started to happen. I found that with every community I met, I learned, I reflected, and I grew...and it cultivated this newfound strength within that made me want more.

If you knew the power of CrossFit, you'd find a group right now too. The world needs more movement and CrossFit gives you an approach beyond anything I've ever seen. If you've ever met a Cross Fitter, they are often quite passionate about CrossFit and don't know how to stop talking about it. If I could, I'd wear a shirt everyday and talk about it non-stop, not just because I love the group, but because of what it's done for my body.

A few things you must know about the power behind this incredible workout...

- CrossFit keeps you moving better daily. It's all about functional movements and these are the things we do often—like sitting, standing, lifting, etc.

- CrossFit workouts are made for EVERYONE. They are scalable and if you find the right gym to learn CrossFit properly, it will change your life. It's all about showing up 3 to 4 times a week to really get the best of what the workout has to offer.
- In life, we want to do everything all at once, however, CrossFit teaches you about the importance of showing up daily to continuously build strength, little by little, over time (this concept is called progressive overload). Building strength overtime with CrossFit has shown to take HUMANS from a place of lack to a place of empowerment with their health.
- You cannot walk into a CrossFit gym with your title in the business world and rock CrossFit. You cannot walk into CrossFit and bring your EGO, or else it will take you out. CrossFit guides you to see your internal power within and let everything else go. I've worked out with some powerful HUMANS in the work world and yet, it didn't stop me from kicking their a** or cheering them on.

We want to be better than yesterday.
We want to be stronger than yesterday.
We want to be healthier than yesterday.

We want to consistently show up for ourselves and watch ourselves get stronger over time.

There is one aspect of the 3Ms I'm asking you to embrace right now—movement with/without CrossFit. Even if you are just starting out, I still suggest CrossFit...

It wasn't the exercise that kept me showing up at yoga, the gym, or CrossFit; it was this powerful sense of what the world needs more of right now—community.

Okay, on to the third and most powerful M of all...the one that gets judged the most and the one that I would yell from the rooftops if more people would tune in and listen...

Marijuana

As I started working out and leaning into the power of mindfulness, my physician at the time opened me up to this powerful opportunity to use medicine as tools.

His words..."accept the pills you are being asked to take...you are at a place that you need them.

However, as you do, learn tools to replace them and over time, work your way off them…"

I had to accept that I needed antidepressants to thrive again. And yet, I knew I couldn't stay on them forever...so as I leaned into new tools, I also chose to explore opportunities outside the realm of pharmaceuticals...

This is where I discovered the powerful medicine that is my third M—marijuana. For me (to this day), this is the ONE consistent M in my life that I've maintained daily and likely will never quit. I find it quite funny that at this stage of my girls' lives they can look at me and say, "Please go have some 'medicine'" (that is what we call weed in our home). When I started, it was difficult to find the right dose for me, but I never gave up trying because I knew that the benefits outweighed the risks.

The right dose is different for every person and it may take some time to find it, but the goal is to balance the brain (more on the science behind this below). It's being able to let go and finally take a deep breath. It's a feeling of relaxation, a higher vibration, and eventually, you can make that state your entire reality. You also won't need to increase your dose to make this reality happen, in fact, if you're doing it correctly you will need to rely on marijuana less and less to find that state again. The more often you find and hold that state, the easier it will come to you, until that is your normal.

Prior to the age of 35, I smoked marijuana twice in my life. I was against it; I judged others for the smell and I was not at all open to its benefits at all. I also had two kids who I couldn't imagine smelling it and saying, "what is that?" It was so much easier to take a pill with no one knowing rather than accept the fact that I may need to open my mind to something very different than I ever imagined I would. With the chronic pain that I was flowing through and the awareness that maybe there was something other than pills that would help, I decided to open my mind. Of all the ways to take weed, the only way that seemed to work for me was smoking it and this realization and acceptance has been one of the hardest to flow with. I had to break down all the judgement I had of others and learn to accept it in myself. I remember in COVID we'd have to line up at the liquor store and having to stand in that cannabis line broke my soul...now everyone would know...now everyone would judge. AS I started feeling different, releasing the judgment of others and welcoming myself to accept what is, I started to see the balance that happened from within and started to feel the superpower that cannabis had on my soul.

To be honest, I've been smoking consistently at night almost daily since 2016 and I would be confident to say that it's been the ultimate healer for my soul.

If the world knew the science on marijuana, the world would not be drinking every day at 4:00 p.m. The world would be taking a puff of this powerful healer and using it as their new tool of choice.

- Did you know that REM sleep increases with marijuana;
- Did you know our bodies are actually made to receive marijuana—there are actually receptors in our bodies that naturally bind to it;
- Did you know that marijuana actually brings your body back to a state of equilibrium—one that very few of us live in right now;
- Did you know that marijuana makes meditation even more mindful;
- Did you know that marijuana can make you become a better parent because you laugh and feel a little more like yourself again;

- Did you know that there is such a thing as not getting so high that you can't function, but microdosing...and this powerful opportunity can guide your body to do magical things.[11]

Microdosing is just a few puffs at a time, starting with just ONE before bed...to sleep better, to feel better...

My pain held me back for a very long time. I could not be a good mom, a good wife, or a good human...

Marijuana allowed me to start seeing that this was possible again and as I embraced it, I was able to let the pills go, all the pills...and now, I am not addicted to marijuana, it's a tool in my toolbox that I call on when I need a little help to get through the day...

These are my 3Ms I choose to do daily and wouldn't have it any other way...

The ultimate power in it all? I found myself again through the power of the 3Ms...maybe today, you will too.

---

[11] The Editors of Mayo Clinic. (2023, Apr. 7). *Medical Marijana: The Science and the Benefits*. Mayo Clinic.

HEART: Mind & Body

What do you like to do for exercise (running, yoga, brisk walking, swimming, biking, etc.)? If you don't like it at least some of the time, you won't do it. Write down a few options here. What have you tried for mindfulness (meditating, gratitude journal, journaling, nature, etc.)? What can you try next? Set an alarm for each activity each day and schedule in 30 minutes of MOVEMENT and 10 minutes of MINDFULNESS to start. Write your plan below.

_____
_____
_____
_____
_____
_____
_____
_____
_____
_____

HEART: Never Have I Ever

Marijuana isn't for everyone AND might not be the right fit for you. Answering these questions will help you to evaluate the potential benefits of changing your current habits. Would you consider using marijuana as a temporary support as you find your way through your trauma to the other side? Have you ever used it recreationally before? How do you think it is different from prescription medication? What else do you use to cope? What emotions typically come with your other coping strategies? Do they really help in the moment or afterwards?

___
___
___
___
___
___
___
___
___
___
___

Chapter 10: Helping Hands

Photo Credit: Alex MacAulay

I used to love being asked for help.

I have always been the helper, the one who wears an invisible shirt that says, "tell me your life story and I'll listen." I am the person found at parties listening to the deepest parts of someone's soul...

I was the one that was there for everyone...

The one everyone counted on, regardless of how hard my day had been or what I've been asked to flow through...

Like so many of us, I always put myself aside...to help.

I did this...until my body YELLED in a way that I had no choice but to listen. I was an EMPTY...BUCKET, toppled over and STOMPED on...

I got sick...and when you get sick...the fear of death takes over and it's incredible what happens...you become scared and that fear drives you to do things differently...

By the time I was at the hospital in 2015, I had hit almost all of the top 10 stressors in life, but I was still helping others! Let me tell you something: the hard never stops, the hard just keeps coming, the hard allows us to see how f*cking resilient we are and no matter how much we try to avoid the hard it keeps flowing. I have literally had to walk away from everything that no longer served me and it left me with nothing. I've gone through floods, I've lost friends, I've lost my husband, I've lost my house, I lost my job, I lost my health. Over the last 3 years there have been many moments when I've sat on the floor and cried, and there have been many moments where I went to my mom's house and said, "I can't do it anymore!" There has been so much unbearable pain. Everything kept falling apart no matter what I did to hold it tight. I am a AAA type personality and over the last 5 years I've become a complete introvert, so that I don't even know how to meet myself some days. I'm quiet, I'm different, but I'm full of happiness and joy. And I don't need to run around showing it to anyone anymore.

I think the hardest thing for me to accept in my life right now is that in order for me to have become the version that I am of myself right now, I've literally had to lose everything, over and over. The concept of attachment has probably become my greatest learning because I realize in attaching myself to anything it becomes almost a sticky slope. Human beings flow, which means that we cannot attach ourselves to anything. The minute that we try to attach ourselves to something, there's an unravelling process to remind us that it isn't possible. Who I've become and who I once was are

> so very different that sometimes I get caught up in the disconnect and get really sad. But then I realize, as we unravel and move forward this is the greatest blessing. I had everything and yet I have chosen instead a path of positivity.
>
>

Who Are You?

What if...

- Who you are is buried under everything that society has taught you?
- Who you are is buried under everything you went through as a child?
- You were shaped by the people you were surrounded by and the stories you have aligned yourself with?
- You have a job/relationship/family title which defines you and yet isn't who you are and doesn't reflect what your soul is meant to be?

So many of us are living what we've become as a result of our 'programming' and we might not even understand what that is. Until.

Something happens to that title…and then we are left wondering…

When I lost my job, that was one moment…then I lost my marriage…and from there all those 'titles' spiralled to the floor and made me take a good look in the mirror, wondering who the f*ck was buried underneath it all…

And yet, as I stopped listening to the noise…and stopped listening to the old opinions of others…and the old stories I created, something else started to shift.

- I started finding moments of mindfulness…
- Mindfulness created space…
- Space created a pattern of flow that wouldn't stop once it started…
- I started hearing the voice within speaking my truth…
- I started HEARing and FEELing the things that actually fuelled me…

- Words that never stopped, patterns that kept yelling...
- The head vs. the heart...
- I started writing...
- I started letting out the shadows...
- The dark side...
- The places I was told to hide...

As I quieted my brain, I noticed that the pain felt different, it became less, I wasn't as triggered...because the pain wasn't so loud, I could hear the messages that the pain was trying to bring...I started feeling compassion and kindness for myself...I started allowing and accepting...and it was one moment at a time.

How did I figure it out? I wrote down my superpowers as a HUMAN...

I am kind...
I am compassionate...
I am love...

I deserve to give these things to myself first...

When I realized who I was and what I was giving away...I knew I had to do something different to ensure I was putting myself first.

These words have guided me tremendously and have become the words I now use to ensure I am putting self first. "I am ready to do this differently" and "I am open to giving and receiving love."

So many of us know how to give love away, but so many of us have no idea how to receive love; yet that is where the magic lives. As emotions have polarities, so does love. If you've shut down your emotions, you've likely turned off the funnel of love from the inside and that is the key to unlocking a way forward. Being open to receiving love is the way your body truly chooses healing, and it's how we truly kickstart self love.

When I became open to receiving LOVE, it felt a bit like anxiety at first. I would get this RUSH of feeling that was uncomfortable, and I would feel my body wanting to go into a curled-up state, wanting to avoid it. And yet, as I learned the power of seeing it differently, I asked my body to receive it differently too. Then I could feel it FLOWING with warmth and the colour green. The colour green is the colour of the HEART chakra, and as I learned to receive love, I would close my eyes. That vibrant green colour would be in my space.

For so many of us, when we make different choices, a feeling of discomfort or anxiety takes over and we react as if it's "bad," which means we receive it as bad. As I started to be more open and welcomed that feeling more often when it arose, I would ask for my body to receive it differently or choose to ask myself, "what if this is LOVE instead of anxiety?" All of the sudden my body would shift. The key to receiving is being open to the sensations that arise without putting a label on them. Allowing them to flow as they are instead of trying to make it logical. The minute we try to understand why something is happening in our body, we immediately go toward LOGIC, but the key to FEELING again is flow, love, and trust which exist in the HEART not the head.

Saying it out loud is also the way your body hears it and when it starts to hear it, it chooses differently.

Now, I love to help again, because my bucket is full...my LOVE is a mirror from within and that alone brings a FEELING of something for which we are all truly worthy.

When we choose us first, HELPing becomes joyful. When we choose us first, LOVE starts the conversation and when LOVE flows through HUMANs, magic happens.

What if today...you made a choice to SLOW down the HELPING and instead HELPED yourself...or even ASKED FOR HELP?

The more we put us FIRST...the more the energy of LOVE flows from within and this my friends...is the SUPERPOWER we've all been searching for!

What Do You Need?

What do you need in times of anger, sadness, and frustration? Is it someone who offers opinions? Or is it someone who listens? Can you even use your words to articulate what you need in HARD times? What do you do with yourself when you are not yourself? Do you get ANGRY at you? Or do you wrap yourself in LOVE and hear what your beautiful, strong, amazing body is asking for?

RECEIVING love means knowing what you need in TIMEs of HARD and choosing to GIVE LOVE to yourself versus. what we so easily give away instead.

What if today, you took one step back from HELPing and instead EMPOWERED your need for HELP? Your need for love? If you don't know how to do this…then I invite you to find out…

Help Yourself

When I made the choice to stop helping others…it was so so so SCARY and I felt so off balance. Those friends I was always there helping stopped calling…my relationship fell apart…my life fell apart because I didn't know HOW to give myself the LOVE I so easily gave away to others. It was scary as F*CK…especially because it happened as I was learning to stand alone. So many of us right now are walking around very empty inside, using things as our way to FEEL better…using HELPING as our strategy of NOT dealing with our own sh*t.

What if today, you heard me out?

When I made the decision to stop helping and instead learned how to both help myself and ask for help, I also learned how to love myself…little by little…moment by moment. My mom always said the greatest words to ever be said are, "I need your help." As I learned to STOP helping and instead learned what I needed to be my best self...what has come is magical.

- I now know what I need to help myself in times of HARD...
- I now know coping strategies that help me when I'm not myself...
- I now have FRIENDS who I can call on to ask for help...

The hardest part of shifting from a HELPER to a LOVER/HELPER of YOURSELF is cracking open your opportunity to RECEIVE love.

SO many of us have NO idea how to RECEIVE LOVE, especially our OWN love.

What does this even mean? It means choosing yourself.

HEART: Self Care

List all the things here that you do solely for yourself. I don't mean something you do for the family that also benefits you. I don't mean something you do out of necessity. What do you do for yourself that is purely for pleasure? You might find that your list is short. Now think of the things that really help you to relax. Add those to the list so you can implement these at some point in the near future. Start doing one thing a week just for you, then add a second one, and then a third. Take note of how you're feeling as you progress. How has your mood changed, your ability to cope? Do you feel like you can handle things better?

_____

_____

_____

_____

_____

_____

_____

_____

_____

_____

_____

＃ Part 6: H.E.A.R.T.

Chapter 11: The 4th "M" is Magic

There is magic within all of us…it comes when we settle our brains and tap into the magic that exists within the love that flows.

Inside all of us are gifts beyond our mind and these gifts are usually very present in early childhood and go away as we let logic kick in and society shapes us. To find your way back, you must take the time to

> go within - to realign your HEART. The hardest part? Not trying to put words to it, not trying to understand it - just learning to be open to what flows when you choose to trust and align with your path. Humans want answers to why. The greatest development of my gifts came when I stopped trying to understand and trusted what my soul was being guided towards. Everyone's gifts are different and your gifts will emerge as you start to flow back to you, to trust yourself, to welcome you to be you - just as you are.
>
>

Messages & Gifts

For me, the messages and gifts have always been present…I could always *feel* people and know their entire life story by looking in their eyes.

- I would see things happening long before they actually did…
- I can see the path of right now…and the path of potential…

- I can see patterns within families and guide others to break them…
- I can sense the pain and anxiety of others…
- I am a mirror reflection and have found it difficult in my life to separate myself from others when I get intertwined.
- I can feel misalignment and it's hard for me to tolerate now that I know…
- I have a keen sense of awareness…
- I have a knowing that is so deep, it's been a powerful feeling and yet hard to accept at the same time
- I see certain numbers often…333 444 555 666 777
- I have words that just come to me…
- I just start singing songs that end up having powerful messages…
- I have people who are placed right in front of me and when conversation flows, I immediately see why…

I can also sense other realms (Humans in Heaven) and other beautiful souls come to me with messages of LOVE and compassion for those who need it most.

My magic hasn't come in just one moment either, it's little moments when the space is created. When the deep stuck emotions start to flow differently and you take the time to pay attention and feel.

Meditation has really allowed me to cultivate this magic and as I watch it play out, it's hard for me to ignore.

My children have guided me to cultivate my magic as they've grown, shared, openly discussed their own moments of magic which has reminded me. Both my girls have an ability to call in those who need help and both my girls see the world of the unknown.

Animals

My animals...I have Harley (cat) and Winston (dog) and they are my everything. They've sat with me when I was sad and they've been there for me in all the moments I had to learn to stand completely alone after divorce. They've been with me while I learned how to love myself unconditionally...50/50 custody is now a blessing, however, when I first had to sit alone Harley and Winston were the 2 souls that kept me company and allowed me to feel, all the while with a sense of LOVE. Animals are healers to humans and great reminders of what unconditional love can bring...they are also superpower feelers, like kids, as their own way forward is only through energy. Harley is an odd cat—always has been—he has sat on my shoulder since he was a little boy, he always wanted to be next to us during dinner and joined me in the bath a few times, falling in while trying to sit on my shoulders. When I meditate and shift my soul to be aligned with higher power, Harley will often find me to help me release the energy. He will come home from outside and start purring to be on my back…to help me feel, to help me flow, and, more importantly, to help me release. He will move up and down my back and sit right where my releases need to happen. When the energy is off in my house or in myself, he gets super grumpy and even nips. I've witnessed him running around chasing energy that I've released, and I've seen him attack me because the energy I've released is yucky to sense and feel. Cats are amazing energy holders…they often sh*t out old energy and for the first 2 years of his life, the sh*t that came out of him was unbelievable…lol. I believe Harley came to remind me of the power of unconditional love…and how wonderful animals can be if you open your heart to LOVE.

Dogs are different, dogs hold energy. I believe dogs hold HUMAN pain…I believe there is a magical superpower between animals and humans however here, I will only talk about dogs. Winston came to me at a time I needed love…the love he has brought has been overwhelming and yet, I wouldn't trade it because it also reminded me of what the movie "A Dog's Purpose"[12] has taught us. I believe Winston is my dad. My dad passed away 3 years ago during COVID and I never really got to say goodbye in person. Since he's left this world, I've felt his presence whenever I've needed it and yet, since Winston has arrived, it's clear my dad is within him. Winston's eyes are human, he winks at me when I ask him about being my dad, and more importantly, when I need strength Winston is there to make sure I feel the strength I need. It is truly remarkable.

Spirituality

My gifts now plus my learnings over my life have guided me to see how powerful we are as humans…life is always guiding us back to who we are really supposed to be. Everything we do out of alignment with our true selves will yell at us…until we flow towards it…if you are sitting in a pile of never ending sh*t, it's time you took a look in the mirror and asked yourself what you are missing.

---

[12] Hallstrom, L. (2017). *A Dog's Purpose*. Dreamworks Pictures. Walden Media. Amblin Entertainment.

When I left my marriage, I experienced the gift of spirituality and source, however, I shut it down because it wasn't something I was comfortable with. As I walked away from my marriage and learned to spend time alone, I saw things I couldn't unsee…

- Times when I met the dead…
- Times when I knew things others didn't…
- Times when I would say something or write something down, and it would happen…

What if, there is always a team surrounding you…of guides, of love, the universe, source—whatever you call it. What if this team is always offering you messages, voices, something…and it's up to you to pay attention, hear its words…how do you do that? You surrender into your HEART vs. hearing your words in your HEAD…you allow…you trust…you open. And the biggest thing you MUST do in order to have their help? Call on them. Actually say out loud, "I need your help to navigate this situation." Your team of supporters can't come forward IF you haven't asked OUT loud for their help.

Full Circle

My mom and I have rekindled and grown our relationship in adulthood in a way that most don't get the chance to do. It has been a true blessing, and my healing journey would NOT be where it is without our unconditional LOVE.

My mom was blessed on her own life path, which like many others was the best at the time. However, in the end, her path also led her to carry core wounds. These core generational wounds become our opportunity if we choose to treat them differently and take the time to go inward. So many of us as adults are angry with the older generation because of the wounds they carried and the actions that followed, and yet carrying this ourselves often results in resentment and anger being carried for life.

Do you know that if you don't choose to heal in the now, that only affects you? Do you know that holding on to anger and resentment eats away at you and makes you—as a parent—act just like your own parents?

As I've come to this powerful awareness, I realize the opportunity we have in the now to flow with our parents—especially our moms—and I've seen magic happen.

I've lost it all as a result of surrendering and welcoming versus forcing and pushing, and the only person who stayed with me the whole time was my Mom. My mom and I have something that is rare. We talk daily and see each other A LOT. I would say, we are almost BEST FRIENDS too.

In COVID, we were blessed to live in buildings that connected and it SAVED us. We spent a lot of time together and I believe we healed together. We learned that the best path forward is only through love.

We talked a lot, we cracked a lot open, and we learned a lot from each other by listening…

My greatest lessons in life have been HEALING with my PARENTS. They all did their best and loved me as much as they were capable. It is not my place to judge that matter, it's the choice I make to accept their love or hold on to the anger and resentment, and to lead my kids down the same path—F*CK NO. So, the time is NOW.

Crack open the MAGIC that is your MOM and DAD, however, know that the bond between MOM and KIDS is far more energetic because of HUMAN NATURE. Moms literally hold children within their bodies for 9 months—children are part of our DNA and body...that knowing, that connection, and that opportunity is also why when we heal with our parents, we open up yet another opportunity to HEAL with our kids.

It really sucks that oftentimes our family dynamic is where we get stuck, how we grew up, and yet we can choose to stay stuck in that or find a different way.

Everyone has their OWN PATH and their OWN PERSPECTIVE and THEIR OWN CHOICES...and if we don't choose differently, the life we have right now is all we will EVER have. It isn't wrong to accept it, however, the path forward will forever be the same and lead you NOWHERE but THERE. These moments of unconditional love, if welcomed, if chosen to release the past and accept it as is, will change you. My time with my MOM, of her reminding me who I am, has welcomed me to come back to me, and be ME again.

It has allowed me to come out of the dark hole that I chose because I was so deeply hurt from the pain that others caused me and yet I allowed them to. Our pain is our greatest gain and my entire life has led me to this moment of unconditional love and acceptance of SELF and it has changed everything.

I always go back to the same quote over and over in my life, from Steve Jobs, "you can't connect the dots looking forward; you can only connect them looking backwards. So, you have to trust that the dots will somehow connect in your future. You have to trust in something—your gut, destiny, life, karma, whatever. This approach has never let me down, and it has made all the difference in my life."

The Voice Within

There's this internal little voice in you and it tells you everything; intuition not ego, heart not head. Here are some ways to tap into the voice within.

I have tapped into the magic that is unconditional love from within. Through deep soul work, meditation, energy healing, and trust, I have found my way toward unconditional LOVE, and I FEEL the universal connection that we all HOLD.

Daily Practices

- Grounding
- Breathwork
- Nature
- Setting Intentions
- Quiet Time

This concept of ONE allows us to already know everything we must to *be* in this world...everything we are and can be is already within us.

I am now so in tune with my body that I feel everything. The trauma that I've faced has led me to sense things I never imagined I could and yet it allowed me to learn how to use my gifts. So many of us have these gifts, however, we go out into the world not knowing and it often overwhelms us.

For me, I believe the voice within—when I'm aligned with my higher self the voice speaks the words of a higher knowing that I am incapable of explaining. Over the years and pretty much my entire life, I've heard this voice and yet I didn't know what to do with it. AS I've done the soul work—taking time to pause and allow—the voice has gotten stronger. The voice has become the guide I've always been seeking...the one that allows me to trust...to be...and more importantly to become. I used to be the control freak, the other who had the plan and executed accordingly—not the voice within, which is the way forward. Now I am doing the daily work to ensure I stay aligned and that's how I flow, knowing that regardless of what I have to face, I will do so because I am aligned.

HEART: Ho'oponopono

"Ho'oponopono is a centuries-old native Hawaiian method of apology and forgiveness still practiced by many...[including] remorse, forgiveness, gratitude, and love."[13] Place your hand over your heart and repeat the words below in order as many times as you need to until you feel your body shift. Sometimes it feels like a yawn, a heavy breath or deep sigh, the release of energy or clearing, a sense of peace–it's an internal knowing that everyone will feel differently, but it's a significant difference in a matter of moments from how your body felt before.

I love you,
I'm sorry,
Please forgive me,
Thank you,
I forgive myself.[14]

---

[13] Sword, R.K.M. & Zimbardo, P. (2021, Nov. 21). Ho'oponopono: "To Make Things Right". The Time Cure. Psychology Today. Retrieved from https://www.psychologytoday.com/ca/blog/the-time-cure/202111/ho-oponopono-make-things-right

[14] Shakti. (2020, May 22). The Power of Ho'oponopono. Medium. Retrieved from https://medium.com/@shakti_yoga/the-power-of-hooponopono-56f6f9c08dcd

Then write down how you feel afterwards. What did your body feel like before and how did it change? Be on the lookout for this feeling to tell you when words ring true because they will tell you something about yourself if you pay attention!

_____
_____
_____
_____
_____
_____
_____
_____
_____
_____
_____

HEART: Authentic Self

What do you do that feels authentic? What is something you do with ease? What is something that comes naturally to you? What did you do as a child that you remember as fun or easy? Something you did without thinking? Make a list here so you can commit to spending more time with these people and doing these things. The more time you spend as/with your true self, the better you will feel!

_____

_____

_____

_____

_____

_____

_____

_____

_____

_____

Chapter 12: Heart First

Photo Credit: Jenny Scott

Today, I am 8 years out from that visit to the hospital and my perspective has completely shifted.

I no longer have the career path of becoming CEO...except for my own life.

I am an amazing mother with 2 beautiful strong girls that mirror who I've become, from the inside out.

I am a superpower feeler AGAIN in my ability to feel and flow through emotions using them as my guide.

I am now a divorced woman with an ex-husband who is my friend and our number one mission is our children.

I am a HUMAN that embraces all aspects of my mind, body, and soul.

I am a cannabis user and now take ONLY one PILL a day to manage my health.

I am a fitness junkie.

I have FIBRO and CFS however they do not define me, they guide me.

Most importantly of all, I am a HUGE believer in myself, and the LOVE I have for myself overpowers everything else.

Brene Brown wrote a quote in one of her books that when I read, I almost vomited and yet it's been my guiding force forward…

"You Cannot Truly Love Others, Until You Love Yourself"

I remember calling bullsh*t on this quote but knowing what I know now and feeling what I feel now, I know she is right. The deeper you love yourself, the deeper your love is for other people. So, you can experience love, but it won't be at its fullest until you fully love yourself. Every time you choose yourself, you are loving yourself. Choosing to walk away from a toxic relationship, choosing a different career path that is more in line with your authenticity, choosing to take care of your body, mind, and spirit. Your capacity to love grows the more you express it to yourself. At first, it may be in looking back where you tend to see these choices the most, but eventually you will get better at recognizing and celebrating your choices in the moment.

My ask after reading my story isn't for empathy or compassion. If any of it resonates with you, I need you to PAUSE and ask yourself right now to do something differently as a result.

Connect

- Find your HEART...
- Choose you.
- Find a way to start small and start choosing you.
- Every day for one moment of the day...
- Do the things that fill you...
- Let go of other people's opinions,
- Let go of what is yelling at you to let go and, more importantly...
- Make space for the things that are meant to flow in...

Find a way to embrace the sides of yourself you aren't listening to...and trust that you are worthy of hearing the words.

THERE IS NO YOU, WITHOUT YOU...and the only choice you have is RIGHT now.

You are welcome to wait for your wake-up call on your health, however, know that if you aren't listening, what may come may scare you so much that you are no longer capable of shifting.

I beg you to tune in. I beg you to make NOW the time you do. You are so f*cking worthy.

Here's how…

I speak a lot about the word HEART…and in my journey I've developed a very simple mindset that may guide you to do the same…

In my learning to FLOW back to my best version of my AUTHENTIC self, I recognized a superpower we all HOLD.

It's quite simple actually. It's not HARD to call on and yet many of us have forgotten about it…or left it behind. Because we are all a little LOST right now…and that's okay. We've been thinking too much in our HEADs…and when we do, it shuts off our HEART form of communication.

What if you knew the HEART isn't just a pump??? What if you knew that your HEART is your body's ultimate guide?

And that EMOTIONS are the language it speaks and WORDS are its SUPERPOWER.

Let's do this exercise together and I'll show you...

Tune In

What if...

- right now you place your HAND on your HEART?
- HOLD it there, take a deep breath in...in through your stomach and out through your chest...while keeping your hand on your heart.
- one more time...just to be sure...remind yourself of a MOMENT of LOVE where you FELT LOVE.
- a moment where you knew love existed, and feel that moment...
- BREATHE it IN...2 deep breaths.
- FEEL the LOVE.
- ASK it to FLOW all around your BODY.
- FEEL the FLOW.
- now, ask the love to surround you and keep you safe as you flow through your day...
- NOW SMILE...and remember how blessed you are.
- CHOOSE to take this FEELING everywhere you go today.

- and when you need it again, put your hand on your HEART and know it's there...
- now before doing ANYTHING ELSE.
- say this OUT LOUD to yourself.
- it's the simple MINDSET of HEART I've created.
- and TODAY, I want to EMPOWER you with it too.

HEART: HUMAN. EMPOWERMENT. ALIGNED RESILIENCE. TRUST.

If emotions are our superpowers, then words are its igniters...whenever I need a dose of HEART, I call on these words...these simple words, said out LOUD keep me flowing and feeling vs. sitting and holding...stand in FRONT of the mirror if you DARE...

"Being HUMAN is my superpower...
EMPOWERING LOVE is my opportunity...
Staying ALIGNED with myself keeps me living true to me...
Drawing on my RESILIENCE makes me FLOW...
TRUSTing I am right where I need to be is how I move FORWARD."

I've got this, [First name "f*cking" Last Name]

As you FEEL these words... know that everyday that you SAY them is a NEW opportunity to do it differently and today... I ask you to pay attention as the SMALL moments of DIFFERENT FLOW in...

Right now, in this world, it's easier to take a look around and see all the external things happening and blame them.

COVID-19 has woken so many of us up in ways we weren't prepared for and now we are all walking around like WTF!

- The plan we had isn't anymore.
- We are different.
- Our kids are different.
- Our relationships are different.
- So many of us have walked away from our marriages.
- So many of us have chosen different careers.
- So many of us have chosen a path of different and yet, we are still holding on to things that really no longer matter.
- SO many of us are learning to stand alone and it's SO HARD.

Everyone is walking around in protection mode…it's like we've all experienced massive heartbreak and instead of dealing with it, we've STUFFED it in. Stuffing is okay in moments…however, if we choose NOT to deal and NUMB instead that is what leads us to where we are right now–off KILTER.

Trust your Gut, Destiny, Life, Karma, Whatever

Remember those words from Steve Jobs? "you can't connect the dots looking forward; you can only connect them looking backwards. So, you have to trust that the dots will somehow connect in your future. You have to trust in something—your gut, destiny, life, karma, whatever. This approach has never let me down, and it has made all the difference in my life."

What if everything we've gone through in the course of our lives is to POP us open to what we are supposed to be vs. what we are running from?

What if this is the universe's way of saying "NOT YOUR PATH"? What if, this is your body's way of saying "IT'S TIME TO DO IT DIFFERENTLY" and I'm going to KEEP GIVING YOU THE SAME SH*T over and over until you CHOOSE TO DO IT DIFFERENTLY?

What if, today, instead of thinking you need to do BIG things to shift, all you did was EMPOWER HEART from within?

Now, more than ever, instead of looking outward at the continuous roller coaster that is life, we are being asked to go inward...to learn how to become more aware of who we are, accept ourselves just as we are, and remind ourselves (right now) that just as we are, is enough.

This is why I PREACH HEART and today I want to EMPOWER you with a simple way to SEE/DO it differently.

HEART is a motto, a mindset...words that shift you quickly. Here is how it works. In moments of HARD, I call on HEART.

HUMAN

I am HUMAN. I make mistakes. I must FEEL the emotion I am being asked to feel: CRY, SCREAM, WHATEVER it is I need to do in that moment and then ACCEPT and LOVE MYSELF MORE…GIVE yourself a GIANT HUG.

EMPOWERMENT

In moments of HARD, I must FLOW through it, not get STUCK in it. What can I do differently NOW? Can I ask for help? Can I empower a different perspective? How can I shift out of this?

ALIGNMENT

Your body knows when it's misaligned–it yells and screams through emotions, feelings, and signs (like red lights when you are in a rush). TUNE in and pay attention right now. Put your HAND on your HEART and feel what it's trying to tell you. Sometimes I ask myself, "Please help me feel this differently."

RESILIENCE

In times of HARD, I don't want to slip back into OLD ways…become the VICTIM or what I call the "ho hum." Today, remind yourself of another moment where you faced something similar and ask yourself "what did I learn?" Can I pull on something from my past that can help? It's likely you've faced this before…and in this pause, it's up to you to see it…

TRUST

There is a GUT feeling within all of us. As kids, our stomachs hurt, as adults, there is this INNER knowing...a truth that just pops up and, TODAY, I am reminding you to TRUST it. Your GUT is right 99 percent of the time. Steve Jobs made all his decisions with his GUT...today, HEAR your GUT'S WORDS and EMPOWER its TRUTHS.

This simple concept for me has shifted everything. In times of HARD, when I call on it as my next step in FEELING and FLOWING, it shifts me almost instantly into something DIFFERENT.

It ALLOWS me always to show up as my best self, from a place of love, regardless of what is going on around me externally.

It WELCOMES me NOT to blame and instead EMPOWERS the responsibility of my CHOICES to take the best ACTION forward for me.

We cannot change others–trust me I've tried HARD– but we can EMPOWER ourselves to see it DIFFERENTLY.

Today, I ASK that you try HEART...remember who you are...that person inside is dying to come out...to show the world.

Stop hiding them and start empowering them differently. When we shift, everyone around us does too...especially our kids and they need all the HELP they can get!

HEART: Love Yourself

What do you love about yourself? Start writing down even small things below and keep adding as you realize how much more you love about yourself!

_____

_____

_____

_____

_____

_____

_____

_____

_____

_____

_____

Conclusion

What if...you can shift it all
By just starting to believe in you...
One small moment a day...
To choose to take the time your SOUL Is begging you for...
To rest, to feel, to PAUSE...
To finally open your mind to seeing things differently...
To TAKE RESPONSIBILITY FOR YOUR ACTIONS
To STOP BLAMING
To see PERSPECTIVE...
To surrender and accept all that you are...
Just as you are...
Regardless of what you've done, said or felt...
To forgive yourself
To discover happiness within
Beyond the mistakes you've made
The sadness you've had to ensure
The pain you've had to feel
What if that pain is here because it's you holding on to the things that no longer serve you...

What if, It's you HOLDING you BACK...
NO one else...
Everything you've had to go through was to get you right here, right now...
You wouldn't be you without it all...
The good, the bad and the ugly...and yet, you are the one HOLDING on to these feelings of shame, of lack and of deeper inner victim mentality...
So, I awaken you today to one powerful opportunity that has shifted it all for me...
CHOICE...
Choice to wake up today and see if differently...
Choice to take action back to you...
Piece by piece, little by little...
Forward...no longer backwards
Towards the light and embrace the darkness
For the darkness keeps us in a loop
The light allows for clarity, for truth
For trust and for an inner knowing beyond what we ever imagined possible.
You cannot have darkness without light however you get to choose the amount of darkness you carry and how you see it
The world needs light, our kids need light, you need light...
Our kids need us to learn how to feel again and this comes from the inside out...

If it starts within us, it immediately translates to our kids...

They are our greatest mirrors remember...

So today I ask you to embrace CHOICE and PERSPECTIVE and to choose to BELIEVE in you AGAIN

Your time is SO NOW

BELIEVE...

The world is f*cking magical on the other side of the darkness you feel...

This is your wake-up call...

Have a magical f*cking life!

Nancy

Photo Credit: New Life Studio

Bonus Chapter: Twin Flame

Do you believe in miracles?

Do you believe in moments you can't explain?

Do you believe in the magic that comes when you ask for something and then it gets delivered in a way you have no words for and changes your entire existence as a HUMAN BEING?

My name is Nancy, and I am a twin flame. Wow...I said that out loud. To say that out loud makes me want to do two things: stand up and be proud of myself for actually admitting it, and yet also cower to the comments that come as a result of speaking a truth that most have no idea how to comprehend. In 2017, I heard the concept of something called a twin flame: "A "twin flame" is a New Age concept that describes a certain intense connection between two individuals who are supposedly 'two halves of one whole.'"[15] A twin flame is one soul that started in this world and eventually became two souls. These souls travel together in the same lifetime, have very similar patterns that they hold within, and yet (when they meet) there is something that triggers within both of them to spiritually unravel in a way that can't be stopped, and literally leaves you left with a completely new approach to life and a knowing that you will never be the same again. To unravel in a way no one is prepared for, which makes you feel crazy lost and yet fascinated by the intensiveness of the connection itself. To just have this deep inner

---

[15] Silva, L. (2023, Sept. 29). Twin Flame: Definition And Signs You've Met Yours. *Forbes Health.* Retrieved from https://www.forbes.com/health/mind/dating-twin-flame/

knowing that they are who you believe they are…and have these super weird…super intense moments that can't be explained to flow through all the things they are meant to, and to heal and come back to unconditional love.

I have always felt different in my ability to LOVE and always knew that something inside me knew that I was meant to find this magical person called the ONE and yet, I had no idea what would come as a result of this belief. As I learned of this concept and started understanding it, I thought it was my husband for a very long time. As I did the work and unravelled what was within me…it was becoming clearer to my soul that it wasn't him, and that this was a pivotal part of unlocking who it was and, more importantly, who I was. I was so fascinated by this belief and also empowered to know that the healing and unravelling of it had to start within me. As I learned to meditate and develop a newfound ability to get super quiet and hear the voice within, it started guiding me to heal.

Now, 4 years later, my twin flame journey has been a large part of the reason I chose to heal as I did. It's

> been the reason I have chosen to really fall deep in love within myself, and it's been the reason I've found my way back to unconditional love and trust in alignment and flow.
>
>

Manifest Destiny

Healing, as we know, isn't one profound moment. It is made up of moments over and over that heal little cracks within and as you allow these cracks to heal with love, moments you can't explain creep in. In 2020 my marriage ended and as I walked away scared sh*tless, I also knew there was a newfound opportunity to find this person the universe called my twin flame...

They say your twin flame comes into your life in a way there is no explanation for and yet how mine happened is profound to say the least. In 2019, I purchased a gym and that gym gave me a community that I am forever grateful for. Within that community were other twin flames–they likely don't know they are–and yet I was beginning to see those of us who are blessed with this gift and why I was chosen for this path.

I remember standing in the bathroom with one of my friends and she flat out asked me "How are you going to find this person?" And I remember looking at her and saying, "he's just going to walk into the gym and I'll just know"...

A week later, he walked in.

And what's crazy is that the night before, I had finally started doing twin flame meditations that would clear my path to allow this moment in time to happen, and the next day it did.

Now, I had no idea who he was…he wasn't my typical type. I didn't notice him, but he noticed me…and apparently when we hugged, he felt something…I felt nothing…

At the time, I really wasn't open to much because I had just come out of my 15-year marriage and really wasn't looking. My gym closed a month later and never reopened due to COVID. Now, looking back, I realize the gym happened for me to meet him. A few months passed after the gym closed and occasionally he'd reach out, asking me for coffee. I had no reason to accept, so I kept putting it off...until one day it happened.

When he showed up, it's a moment I still have no words for to this day. Every time he shows up, it's like time stops and the intensity of it causes both of us to be amazed pretty much every time...

WE sat that day for about an hour and yet it felt like a lifetime, and when he got up to leave it was a moment that is forever imprinted in my soul. When you meet your twin flame, a deep knowing takes over...there is no explanation for what happens. It is just a moment in time that shifts your soul forever.

That day as he stood in my front hall, something happened. He stood there and spoke my soul's truth. He stood there and pretty much told me my journey without me having to say words and at the end he said, "You've been calling me here, and I am here for you to learn how to trust again."

WTF...

I remember standing there, and my third eye chakra (this is our intuitive knowing) was going off in a way that all I wanted to do was sit in the corner and go…am I f*cking crazy or did that just happen? What is your third eye you ask? It's our intuitive knowing, the one that keeps knocking us over the head with moments, or messages, or things you can't understand. For me, that day, it felt like my soul wanted to come out of my forehead…it felt like a light literally beaming and connecting with his soul in a way that I truly have no words to describe, except POWERFUL. My entire being as a HUMAN changed—and, in that moment, I didn't have a choice. I had to choose an entirely different path forward.

Lighting the Fire

After that moment, I started unravelling things that I can't explain. As I sat that evening in complete AHHH…I cracked the knowing that he was it…and yet meeting him led to a spiritual unravelling for which I have no words and multiple falls to the ground for both of us to see clarity on what this was…

We didn't do well in our first attempt at being together…there was old baggage in the way, and if you know the twin flame journey, you know that oftentimes it leads to heavy stuff emerging between the two of you and separation because it's just too intense. We were together for the first time for six months–it became clear we both had healing to do–and in the end, we made a choice to separate because it was just too hard at that moment in time to make it work.

Over that six months, it was crazy to me to be able to FEEL him…we'd only be together for a few hours a week and yet it was almost as if he'd never leave my body…

- His touch…
- His feel…
- His words…
- His SMELL…

It was like he'd taken over my soul and there was no way to comprehend what was happening. Every time I'd meditate, he would come to me…we would almost speak…in my sleep, he would be with me…and whenever I needed him, I'd put my hand on my HEART…and there he was…

Nothing felt the same after his arrival…our moments together were intense. He'd always sit in the chair across from me and above the chair was the word HOME…

When we'd sit together and touch–time didn't matter and the depth of what we felt just couldn't be described. The universe aligned with us and started giving us both signs…synchronicities and everything you could imagine to f*ck with my mind over this situation. They say that twin flames are mirror reflections of one another and f*ck, this was the hardest mirror reflection for my soul to face, especially at a time where I wasn't ready to feel the intensity of what was being shared.

Six months later, it was over.

Magic, Miracles, & Love

After our meeting and separation, I made a commitment to stop being so specific about what I was manifesting and instead align with the Universe. Even though I felt my knowing of being a true twin flame, there were also so many doubts. Instead of remaining very specific in my ask, I instead try to align with words that would attract what was RIGHT for me. My words became "Magic, miracles, and love." I wrote them every day for a year and what came truly continued to blow my mind.

"Magic" flew in as a soul mate…another chapter that my HEART was calling me to follow. At first it felt right, however, within a few months, something odd started happening and yet I knew I had to trust…I felt like I was starting to go crazy…

My twin flame and his energy was creeping in…

How is it that you feel something as intensely as I did…and yet there was no communication to confirm what I'd been feeling…

- I would wake up and feel him…and fall asleep at night feeling him…
- I would hear his words and thoughts and I also could see his whole future…
- It was even crazy that as we parted ways, I took his energy and manifested his illnesses within me…
- No matter what I did and how much I tried to run from it, the energy and the feelings wouldn't stop…

I know...reading this you are probably like. "WTF, Nancy!"...and yet, here I was. At this point, I really felt crazy and started speaking to people who weren't my people. Friends who I thought were my friends and yet they weren't. The people that weren't meant to hear my words. The people that no longer resonated with my next chapter, who made me feel crazy, who made me feel like I was losing my mind...

And yet, this little voice inside me kept telling me to trust...so I did. As I continued on this incredible journey, I started to see the path that I needed to follow...

- The "MAGIC" of my gift...
- The magic of being me...and accepting myself as a twin flame...
- In order to move forward in this journey...
- I had to go deep within myself...
- And heal the parts of me that needed love...
- And allow the part of me that felt incredible unworthiness to come out...
- To be felt...
- To be welcomed...
- To be seen differently...

And when I would lose faith or see a mirror reflection I didn't like, I had to sit back, reflect, and allow myself to get clarity on why…to trust the reflection and accept the message it was showing me. The key to this journey isn't to focus on your twin–it's to focus on healing yourself back to unconditional love and connecting back with SOURCE or HIGHER power…

Second Attempt

Once you meet your twin, you cannot veer from them.
Trust me, I've tried. Over and over and over…
It's a soul bond that never parts…
You can let go and it will find a way to creep back in…
You can make peace and it will find a way to flow in…
No matter what, it never parts…

So, instead of running, I made a choice to lean in and allow myself to trust this weird feeling. My friend recommended a book *Calling in "The One": 7 Weeks to Attract the Love of Your Life* by Katherine Woodward Thomas. I started it in October and my mission was to call him back by Christmas.

- Every single day, I did the book and its exercises…
- Every single day I'd pray…
- And the universe started giving me these moments in which I had NO words…
- For the first time in about a year, I passed him in his truck…
- There was one day that we passed each other and time stopped as we drove by one another…
- I can still close my eyes and FEEL that moment….

The turning point in it all…was December 24th. I had asked the universe to bring him HOME by Christmas and on December 24th…out of the blue…he asked me for tea. When I asked him why he asked, he had no words, and yet deep down I knew his truth. This was our first time speaking in almost a year, and when I asked him about morning and night…he confirmed that's when he'd think of me as well…

Now, that moment didn't bring us back together…these last two years have been what many of us twin flames experience…

- The push and pull…
- The never-ending overthinking…

- The separations…
- The old baggage that never stops emerging…
- And yet, one thing is for certain now within both of us…
- We know who we are for each other…
- We know we can never part…
- We know that regardless of what has been, the universe will find a way to bring us back together…

And no matter how often we part, we always come back different and more open to trusting the path. In the two years since that Christmas…what has happened can't be explained.

We've parted ways over and over because we continue to be misaligned…and yet the universe finds a way to realign our paths…sometimes five days in a row in the same spot. I'll walk away and start dating because I get frustrated and within two dates it's over, and then he pops back in out of nowhere. I literally can't date anyone else…I go on dates, enjoy the first few moments together, and then something happens and it's just over…like crazy things…moments you can't explain…extreme deal breakers…intense drama. And within hours of it ending, my twin flame reaches out…and hasn't reached out the entire time…

Last Christmas, the day after I stopped dating this man, I walked into the grocery store, felt his presence, and poof–there he was. We won't talk for a few weeks and someone will recommend a book and his name is in it…(his name isn't common). We will close the chapter, even block each other, and then one day we both click back, and it's like it never happened. We have this ability to forgive each other based on a connection that no matter what happens, the moment I shift or grow out of old, he comes in differently too…

As the mirror has shifted and profound moments have made us crack this entire situation, it's now clear to both of us that we are ONE and we are meant to be together in this world.

I cannot tell you the pain I've had to endure in this journey of trust…I've literally had to fall to the ground over and over to rise differently and yet, here I am…

My twin flame and I aren't together in marriage yet…all I know is that writing this chapter will be the final piece that my soul needs to allow it all to come together as it should.

The most fascinating thing for me was watching myself do more prayer, surrendering more to the power of the universe, and seeing how it divinely brought him in as I did...more texts...more reach outs...him doing things differently...him showing up, saying the words he'd speak to me in my HEAD during meditation. The twin flame journey is solely about unconditional love and rediscovering self. All I know is that as I did the work, he came closer...and that alone has given me faith.

Faith. Trust. Alignment. Union.

Law of Attraction

On top of the knowing and growing together, what's also been crazy for me is the number of people that I've met since, who are one of the same...a twin flame. We get talking about spirituality and all of a sudden, they too announce they are a twin flame. And as we sit and have no words for our journeys, we find peace in the knowing that at least we aren't alone. The journey for me has been about unconditional love and finding it so deeply within my own soul that nothing can take me away from the deep inner knowing that I am right where I am supposed to be. Trusting what is. Believing in this knowing and not losing sight of the amazing magic that exists within all of us if we choose to believe.

So now the people around me are no longer the people that can't hear my words…they are also one of the same…twin flames.

After all of this journey…LOVE is what is here…right now…in this moment. The unconditional love that I've developed in myself in these last few years has been soul healing. The inner healing I've done for myself has been powerful and the only KNOWING I have right now in this world is that as long as we travel together, aligned in our knowing, things will never be the same again. I love differently…I feel differently…and more importantly this journey has been the greatest blessing (and curse) I've ever experienced.

HEART: Twin Flames

Who are the people that keep coming back into your life regardless of major transition or change? Who are the people that you are aligned with in your heart and on your journey? Who is here on this planet to challenge you to be better? Who can you be your complete and full self with? Use this exercise to determine who you would like to keep close in your life to help you on your journey towards HEART.

_____
_____
_____
_____
_____
_____
_____
_____
_____
_____

Nancy Seibel

The Nancy Perspective

Psychic? Intuitive? Soul Feeler? Path Clearer?

I speak soul. I disregarded my gift for a very long time. I am blessed to see the paths you can't see clearly, and my goal is to empower you with the opportunity to do life differently. Our conversations are SOUL healing, regardless of how long we talk for.

Who am I? Why do you need me to help you?

I was a triple A personality with a drive for success. I came out of my Human Resources/Business Degree at the University of Western ready to conquer the world in business. I started my career in Publishing and discovered that sales was my expertise as my **innate ability to connect with humans** is incredible. From publishing, I followed in the family footsteps and went to Pharma where my career took off. I was the National Trainer for Woman's Health and knew that my career path was well on its way to becoming the CEO one day in my life...but my body and soul had other plans. My wake-up call was a health crisis that could only be addressed by turning all of the energy I was giving everyone else back on me. It was the greatest turning point of my life.

Not only did I heal me, but I also healed my kids too. I unravelled the chaos I had created in the first 5 years of their lives and have shifted their paths too. Through discovering self love within, my kids now mirror the same and show up as their best selves too. I lost a lot in my healing journey—my marriage and my career path—however I found myself and a new story to move forward with. I now possess incredible superpowers which flow from unconditional love. The story I am creating now, is powerful, strong, and may be **the key you need to do the same.**

I am no different than you sitting here reading this! My wake-up call brought me back to a place of love, compassion and kindness that I didn't know existed within and now I choose to share my learnings with others.

Our time together promises to wake up your soul. Together we connect. Together we share. Together we empower. **The choice is all yours,** I am only your guide. The time is now, and now, more than ever, you are so worthy of healing, change, and love.

Qualifications

I have my Bachelor of Commerce degree in Human Resources Management and Services from Western University. Through my career path I have enjoyed roles in Real Estate, Pharmaceuticals, as a Sales Representative, and a National Trainer. In 2015, I took a step back from my career path to be a mom to 2 beautiful girls. During this time off, I developed a strong passion for personal development and fitness, becoming certified as a CrossFit and Mindset Coach and actually taking ownership of a CrossFit gym for several months.

I achieved my Life Coaching Certificate from the Centre for Applied Neuroscience in 2016 and am shifting my career to focus on spiritually-guided life coaching. I am also certified in Reiki (Level 2), Body Talk (Level 1), Past Life Regression, Adult Education, and the Science of Self Empowerment.

Get in Touch

I offer one-to-one sessions, group workshops, and motivational presentations to help others find their true selves and move forward with their lives. I have been there, navigated through, and am blessed with amazing spiritual gifts that I use to empower and uplift others on their journey.

It will be my pleasure to meet you!

Nancy F*CKing Full of Love Seibel
Spiritual Guide & HEART Coach
BComm Human Resources, Life Coach, Certified Reiki Practitioner
The Nancy Perspective
thenancyperspective@gmail.com
www.thenancyperspective.ca

Resources

Carey, N. (2012, March 6). *The Epigenetics Revolution: How Modern Biology is Rewriting Our Understanding of Genetics, Disease, and Inheritance*. Columbia University Press.

Dispenza, J. (2019, March 5). *Becoming Supernatural: How Common People are Doing the Uncommon*. Hay House, Inc.

Doidge, N. (2015, Jan. 27). *The Brain's Way of Healing: Remarkable Discoveries and Recoveries from the Frontiers of Neuroplasticity*. Penguin Life.

Hay, L. (2016, March 22). *Mirror Work: 21 Days to Heal Your Life*. Hay House, Inc.

Lipton, B. (2015, Oct. 13). *The Biology of Belief: Unleashing the Power of Consciousness, Matter, and Miracles*. 10th Anniversary Edition. Hay House, Inc.

Mate, G. (2011, Feb. 11). *When the Body Says No: The Cost of Hidden Stress*. Vintage Canada.

Nelson, B. (2019, May 7). *The Emotion Code: How to Release Your Trapped Emotions for Abundant Health, Love, and Happiness*. St. Martin's Essentials.

Neufield, G. & Mate, G. (2011, Nov. 30). *Hold On to Your Kids: Why Parents Need to Matter More Than Peers*. Vintage Canada.

Ratey, J.J. (2008, Jan. 10). *Spark: The Revolutionary New Science of Exercise and the Brain*. Little Brown Spark.

Sachs, N. (2023). Understand Chronic Pain. *The Cure for Chronic Pain.*
https://www.thecureforchronicpain.com/understanding-your-pain

van der Kolk, B. (2015, Sept. 8). *The Body Keeps the Score: Brain, Mind, and Body in the Healing of Trauma*. Penguin Books.

Winfrey, O. & Perry, B.D. (2021, April 27). *What Happened to You?: Conversations on Trauma, Resilience, and Healing*. Flatiron Books.

Woodward Thomas, K. (2021, May 11). *Calling in "The One" Revised and Expanded: 7 Weeks to Attract the Love of Your Life*. Harmony.

www.ingramcontent.com/pod-product-compliance
Lightning Source LLC
Chambersburg PA
CBHW051544020426
42333CB00016B/2084